THE SEVEN STAGES OF SUCCESSFUL UNEMPLOYMENT
From Hell to Hallelujah!

By Steven Zipkoff

©2004 Steven Zipkoff

All rights reserved. No part of this book may be reproduced or transmitted in any form or by any means, electronic or mechanical, including photocopying, recording, or by any information storage and retrieval system without permission in writing from the publisher.

Illustrations by Alvin Blick.

Published by FIRST FLIGHT BOOKS
A division of Bruce Bendinger Creative Communications, Inc.
2144 N. Hudson • Chicago, IL 60614
(773) 871-1179 FX (773) 281-4643
www.firstflightbooks.com
www.successfulunemployment.com

Printed in the United States of America

1 2 3 4 5 6 7 8 9 10

ISBN 1-887229-19-1

Dedication

I dedicate this book to my guideposts – those individuals who have had a major impact on my life and career: my parents, Jack and Rose Zipkoff; my loving wife Barbara, who is still my major support system after 36 years of marriage; and my daughters Sherie Wigder and Jamee Zipkoff, both of whom made sacrifices when needed to ensure our family would survive the unexpected dangers that have a tendency to pop up when you least expect them.

Contents

Editor's Warning
Don't say we didn't warn you.   vii

Preface
Some encouraging words.   ix

Acknowledgements
Don't forget to thank all the people who helped you.   xii

Introduction
Some observations on the world we live in.   xv

Prelude
Life lessons learned from the *Wall Street Journal*.   xvii

Welcome to Hell!
What you need to be aware of and how it feels when unemployment surfaces and bites you in the…   2

The U-Zone
Don't let unemployment immobilize you.   18
The Seven Stages – A Preview.   22

Stage One… Putting up a Positive Front
Unemployment is a positive adventure. Learn how to develop a positive attitude.   31

Stage Two… Accepting the Fact
Accept the fact, take control of your life and your situation. Begin today… or tomorrow.   40

Stage Three...
Developing the Résumé
Develop a résumé that places you above the competition.   55

Stage Four...
Getting Your Unemployment Benefits
Required action to receive your windfall of money.   70

Stage Five... Creating a Plan
Develop a plan and move forward. Find your
new opportunity.   84

Stage Six... Making It Happen
Master the intricate art of networking in order to
find your new job or opportunity.   97

Stage Seven... Hallelujah!
You've found your new opportunity. Don't forget
what you went through. And don't forget those
who helped you.   153

Final Thoughts
I hope you've had enough… on to success!   162

Editor's Warning

On their way to becoming a "practical guide," Steve Zipkoff used these pages as therapy to help him through his own difficult time.

The practical tips and advice Steve developed and shares with you are often interrupted by extended rants that demonstrate how crazy you can get when you enter "The U-Zone."

The good news is Steve worked his way through it – and so will you. So if some of his delusional, smart-alec, this-would-be-funnier-if-it-wasn't-me-on-my-ass humor sounds like you feel – well, at least you know that:

    a) you aren't alone; and

    b) you'll get over it.

We hope you enjoy reading this book – and if you don't, at least it's a whole lot shorter than *Lord of the Rings*.

– **The Editors**

Preface

Unemployment is not a new phenomenon.

It has been around since man developed the concept of work (actually, unemployment was invented the next day), and it will be around as long as man continues to work.

Along with unemployment comes a wide variety of books to teach you how to become employed again. Every book has its own special method with its own special advice and flair.

So what makes this book so unique? Well, for one thing, it is written by me. So much for the flair part.

Then again, I'm a person who has actually experienced the pain and suffering of unemployment. I vividly remember what it felt like when I learned I was "out of a job," regardless of the reason. It's a feeling, I might add, that I hope I never experience again. So far so good.

I also remember what it was like to go on job interviews and be rejected over and over again.

"You don't meet our qualifications."

"You don't have enough experience."

"You don't come from our industry."

"You lack industry knowledge."

"You're too qualified for the position."

"Steve, we'd really like to hire you, but we simply can't afford to pay you what you're worth."

The list seemed endless. I'd get at least one per interview.

I also remember the panic attacks.

These come along with unemployment free of charge. You think you will never get another job because "many positions in your career area have been eliminated permanently."

I was scared to death when I realized that the money I had saved for other purposes – a family vacation, a new car, retirement, etc. – now had to be used to survive. And over and over again, the worst feeling of all, "what if I can't find a job?"

You can't ignore all these feelings and concerns, but I can tell you this; once you realize that unemployment is only temporary and that, by having a positive attitude, an enthusiastic behavior, and a relentless persistence to succeed, your job or opportunity hunt will proceed more positively. And you will be rewarded with a new job or business venture. You will.

Even if you have encountered a variety of roadblocks – a limited number of job interviews, not enough job openings, résumés sent out by the thousands with minimal response, countless reasons for not being hired – understand that this is not uncommon. When you go fishing you must put chum (bait) in the water to attract fish. You must do it often and not only use lots of chum, but it has to be the right type at the right time for the fish you're fishing for. The same holds true when searching for that new exciting opportunity.

You must use a wide variety of methods to find your new opportunity. You must talk to everyone you know – leave no stone unturned.

Remember, every no you get brings you just a bit closer to the yes you desire and so desperately want.

Once I identified what I wanted to do for the rest of my life, I relentlessly pursued it. You must do the same thing.

Hopefully, this book will help you get through the pain of unemployment and help you move positively through your own seven stages of successful unemployment.

Once you begin to realize that it is entirely up to you to succeed, and once you begin to develop an effective plan of attack, guess what…you *will* succeed.

So start reading and get moving.

The positives are waiting for you.

You have a new life and new adventures just over the horizon. Don't let them pass you by.

Acknowledgements

Like very fine wines (and now I can afford them again), I believe book acknowledgments are extremely valuable and shouldn't be handed out willy-nilly.

For me they represent the sincere thanks to a few special individuals who have been invaluable to me as I became successful both in business and in unemployment.

First, my wife Barbara. Without her support during these periods of my life it would have been difficult to manage and maintain my sense of humor. When you are unemployed, the support system surrounding you becomes increasing important. She was the leader of the pack and a valuable sounding board. We have been married for more than 35 years. That doesn't happen without a lot of sacrifice and understanding.

Second, my fabulous daughters, Sherie and Jamee. They lived through the seven stages and were smart enough to realize that sometimes sacrifices had to be made. They accepted them with minimal complaints. The attitudes of your family are the building blocks of successful unemployment. My two daughters were a major part of that foundation. Also, a world of thanks to my son-in-law, Jeff, who was kind enough to marry Sherie and take her off my family payroll.

Third, my mom, Rose. It is her attitude and vibrant sense of humor while I was growing up that provided me with the drive to be successful and to be able to cope with almost anything life has been able to throw at me and my family. At this writing, she is now 96 and still can make me laugh.

Fourth, my brother Barry and sister-in-law Suzanne. They are vital key players in my support system. My brother, an independent entrepreneur, gave me the advice to go out and start a business and stop depending on others. "All they can do is deter your progress." OK, maybe he didn't say it exactly like that, but I'm sure that's what he meant. In addition, they were an important financial resource that we were able to rely on when things began to become slightly stressful.

Fifth, my mother-in-law, Ilse. That's right, I'm acknowledging my mother-in-law. Not only did she furnish my wife, but her chocolate chip cookies became sustenance when tuna helper became more than we could handle.

Finally, my thanks to all the companies that continue to re-organize, re-focus, re-tool, re-position, and re-engineer so that the number of unemployed people is larger than ever before.

If it wasn't for your lack of planning and strategy and your sometimes stupidity, I wouldn't have such a large audience to appeal to with this book. Not to mention the fact that if it wasn't for you, I probably wouldn't have had the time to write this book, because I was a product of these "re" strategies to begin with.

Introduction

Today, most working Americans are living with a potential dark cloud over their heads... *unemployment.*

As companies, restructure, reorganize, retool, refocus, reposition, and reengineer, they're distributing more pink slips than Victoria's Secret.

Employees are being laid off, fired, cut back, reduced in number and downsized.

And it's getting worse.

Add in mischievous accounting practices, unscrupulous top management, take-no-prisoners competition, and a pressure on corporations to make a profit that is more demanding than ever. This places a strain on both the company and the employee. After all, one sure way to reduce costs is to reduce the number of employees.

And that's the world in which we live and work.

That's why I've written this book, a sometimes humorous book about a serious subject.

It's designed to educate, instruct, motivate and entertain.

It's a travelling companion to help you journey through the seven stages of successful unemployment on the way to a new career opportunity, whether it's your journey or that of a friend or family member.

xv

The marketplace has changed dramatically over the past several years, but the effect of unemployment hasn't.

It's still a devastating experience for you, your spouse, your family, friends, former fellow workers, and others. And it's getting worse (did I mention that?). The unemployment environment is shaking the foundation of our culture.

This is a book describing unemployment from the sometimes humorous view of someone who has experienced this situation.

It describes how you should go about finding a new opportunity. It offers some hope that being unemployed can be less stressful than you imagine. And it tells you you're not alone.

Being unemployed, although very personal, is not an isolated situation. In fact, most workers have been unemployed at one time or another. And if they haven't, they will be. "It's just a matter of time."

The seven stages of successful unemployment are: putting up a positive front, accepting the fact, developing the résumé, getting your unemployment benefits, creating a plan, making it happen, and hallelujah. Each chapter describes each stage and explains how you can traverse the stage to find a better new job or career opportunity.

Now sit back, relax, begin reading, and enjoy as you begin to move through each stage safely and with minimal stress to achieve your ultimate goal…a new opportunity.

Steven Zipkoff • Dallas 2004

Prelude

In June 1998, after six years of being on my own as a management educator, Hal Lancaster of the *Wall Street Journal* wrote an article about my career.

The article was titled "Life Lessons: Learning from a Long Career That Had Lots of Turns." My career did not follow the typical career path of a business executive, and he felt people could learn from my experiences.

There are a number of great learning points that I developed throughout my career, and I feel you might benefit by being aware of them. Following is a reprint of that article.

I'm reprinting it because I believe if you learn from these lessons, life might be a little easier, especially during a period of unemployment. Maybe you can relate to them yourself.

Managing Your Career

Life Lessons: Learning from a Long Career That Had Lots of Turns

by Hal Lancaster

Steve Zipkoff started his career pursuing the road less traveled. Now, it looks more like a well-worn path, even with all the twists and turns.

While he craved a management career, he eschewed an MBA, opting instead for undergraduate and graduate degrees in marketing and advertising from the University of Illinois.

In the 1970s, while others sought security with a single employer, he hopped from job to job in pursuit, frankly, of more money.

His hopscotch approach eventually made it harder to find new jobs. "A lot of people looked at my résumé and said, 'We can't use you – you'll leave in two years,'" he says. "I wasn't smart enough to figure out that the more you did this, the worse it became."

Mr. Zipkoff has faced myriad challenges in his search for a comfortable and happy work life, which ended when he decided to strike out on his own.

He was fired by one employer, left another a step ahead of a restructuring, and hit a plateau when he wouldn't leave Dallas for family reasons. He also dabbled in a short-lived start-up and was unemployed for a year.

Here are some of the life lessons he picked up on his journey:

LESSON 1:
Prepare for the worst

Mr. Zipkoff tells corporate clients to prepare contingency plans for anything that would have a devastating impact, even if it isn't imminent. He has managed his career the same way. While hopping between marketing jobs with Foote, Cone & Belding, Sears, KFC, Burger King (twice), Taco Bell, and I Can't Believe It's Yogurt, he always tried to anticipate change. When Burger King was sold to Grand Metropolitan in 1988, he expected the sale and the layoffs. So when he was offered a car, health benefits, and six months salary to leave, he gratefully accepted and started the new job he had already lined up.

"When companies merge or bring in big consulting companies you'd be a blithering idiot to think it won't affect you," he says.

He endured a year of unemployment after quitting in 1989 as marketing director for I Can't believe It's Yogurt, a Dallas-based chain of yogurt shops, because of "style differences." Despite having a mortgage and two kids in college, he remained confident in his abilities. Besides, he had always lived modestly, driving a 1987 Honda and living in a 2,400-square-foot home. "If you live at or below your means," he advises, "you can survive something negative."

LESSON 2:
Humor will get you through anything

While job-hunting, Mr. Zipkoff decided to write *I've Become an Expert...Damn It*, a humorous account of his unemployment.*

The book was not written initially with publication in mind, but it was a form of therapy that kept him going.

LESSON 3:
Who you know is still more important than what you know

While a regional marketing director for Taco Bell in 1985, Mr. Zipkoff says he initiated the company's first low-priced menu, which boosted revenue and profits in his region.

But a year later, Mr. Zipkoff was fired for poor performance.

He says it was for political conflicts that began when he was accused of ignoring the chain of command in creating the new pricing campaign.

Taco Bell spokesman Peter Stack says the company couldn't immediately locate Mr. Zipkoff's personnel records, but that the low-priced menu was an innovation of former chairman John Martin.

While such a sacking might have hurt his chances with some employers, Burger King, the company he had left to join Taco Bell, rehired him as a division marketing director almost immediately. Why? Because the hiring manager had worked with him previously and "knew my record," Mr. Zipkoff says.

---

* *I've Become an Expert...Damn It* was changed to *The Seven Stages of Successful Unemployment! or... From Hell to Hallelujah.*

The Taco Bell experience, among other things, soured him on the politics of corporate life. "If your boss is doing well, you generally do well," he says. "If your boss isn't doing well, you're in trouble."

LESSON 4:
Don't get pigeon-holed

Mr. Zipkoff chafed at the labels corporate employers hung on him. Employers outside the fast-food industry had a hard time relating his experiences to their businesses. "My performance had always been good," he says, "but it wasn't moving me where I wanted to be."

So he launched Zipkoff Consulting Services in 1992, specializing in strategic planning and "revenue regeneration."** He earns a good six-figure income, more than he ever had before, and at age 54, professes to be happy at last. Also, he boasts, he doesn't have a single fast-food client.

LESSON 5:
Give and you shall receive

If Mr. Zipkoff's final bill exceeds his estimate, he says, "I eat the difference." He also conducts free workshops for customers. He enjoys these acts of good will, but also hopes the exposure attracts new business. "I'm not Mother Teresa," he says. "But I worry about the payoff later; there's always a payoff."

** *In 1999, I changed the company name to Zipkoff Solutions to reflect more of what I was offering clients. We still operate by that name today.*

There better be, since he gets paid by the project. How does he live with the insecurity? "I'm very comfortable," he says. "My security depends on my performance, nobody else's."

LESSON 6:
Opportunities come in the strangest guises

While waiting for a table at the Original Pancake House one morning, Mr. Zipkoff struck up a conversation with an old man to whom he had given his seat. That old man turned out to be an influential former Dr. Pepper executive who referred Mr. Zipkoff to his first client. "You never know when the next business opportunity will come," he says.

The Book Begins...

Welcome...

We begin by dreaming possible dreams... but then find ourselves rudely awakened as we discover the reality check is in the mail!

The sun was shining brightly on the small tropical isle. OK, it wasn't a small island; it was a large one. Big deal. What's the difference?

The difference? Easy. You're not here.

It was a clear January day. The water was as blue as the deep sky where the sun floated overhead. My body floated below. The sun felt good on my body as I stretched out on this nearly deserted part of the beach.

I'd been looking forward to this holiday for the past two years. Things were finally going well at the office, and the company was making more money than we had ever projected. Not bad, considering the company was in tremendous financial difficulty just a few years ago. Life couldn't be better.

(Well, maybe it could be, but this is my dream and I say things couldn't be better. You want to have your own dream, go ahead. This dream was mine. Life was great.)

It was great to lay back and relax after all those days at the office. The long hours were all worthwhile. The company was succeeding beyond our wildest imagination.

Now it was reward time.

My life had a lot of rewards. A loving wife. Family. Money in the bank, nice big house, and the Mercedes was paid for.

We were beginning another phase in our drive through life.

The kids had moved away. Well, not permanently.

They were in college. This means they still had a direct financial pipeline to our bank. Per contract, they would call once a week to check up on us and their money.

One would call at the drop of a hat. She was the one who went away to college in state. She liked being near the family – far enough away so we couldn't check up on her social life, but close enough to drop in on ours.

The other daughter moved far away. I think she picked the school she would attend by getting an atlas and selecting the school that was the farthest away in actual land miles but still featured English as the primary language.

3

So she selected the University of Alaska at Anchorage. (Eskimo is the second language.) You should see our phone bills.

It was time for Barbara and me to slow down and catch up after years of striving and surviving. Sound familiar? The good news was we were still both young enough to enjoy it.

We'd known each other for most of our lives. Going to the same schools as children, we just assumed that when we were older, and of course wiser, we would get married. We did. And we are still married. Happily.

I thought we were a pretty good-looking couple. The strange part of this entire relationship was that I was (am) extremely outgoing, while she was slightly on the introverted side. Friends who knew us as we grew up thought that our marriage would last approximately six months to a year. Recently, we celebrated our thirty-sixth anniversary.

Barbara is a teacher. She had just completed another session of teaching summer school. My image of that session was her with a class of juvenile delinquents taking math for the third time so that they could get enough information to begin robbing banks. I guessed math was also important for this group because it gave them the knowledge to figure out what numbers to select while trying to win the state lottery or trifectas at the racetrack.

My wife was dedicated to ensuring that our young people progressed down the road of life.

But every road has a turn or two. Mine was ready to hit a pothole of epic proportion.

An Interruption… This Can't Be Good

"Steve," *a voice said softly, "are you with us? If you want to daydream, this is not the place. We are in a state of crisis, and we need your full attention."*

It certainly didn't sound like my wife. It wasn't. It was Ralph, our illustrious company president, the person who put us in our current state of crisis management. Well, so much for the beach, the sun, and the solitude. I blinked my eyes…

Ralph was the type of guy everyone liked. A young, industrious entrepreneur, he'd literally give you the shirt off his back, if he was able to buy it wholesale.

And if he was assured he'd get two shirts in return.

Ralph had been a small, successful businessman all his life, dabbling in all sorts of ventures. Small restaurants, real estate holdings, local banks, and an assortment of gimmicks and opportunities that added up to quite a fortune.

Unfortunately, this fortune was based on the fact that his wife was a gas passer – literally – and her family had amassed a fortune in the ether business.

Born in Europe in the late '30s, we're not sure where, Ralph came to America with the dream all immigrants have…make a great deal of money and live happily ever after.

For Ralph, it was a reality.

Gazing out the window overlooking Lake Fred (no kidding), one found it hard to believe that the company Ralph and I built over ten years was about to collapse into financial ruin.

I thought about the good things we'd done.

We'd built the company from scratch, and those first years, sales and profits looked pretty good.

But things began to change, and now we were contemplating our fate. The outlook was not promising.

Once profitable, now we were on the verge of financial ruin. As the economy went south, so did our business.

Customers were no longer in our restaurant. Obviously, a lack of customers is not a good sign.

We were looking at a business with limited sales volume and a bank debt that would make any bank official nervous. "This is not good," I thought. It's thoughts like this that made me a valuable executive.

How did the business get like this? Well, like many executives facing difficulties, we blamed factors outside our control; i.e., increased restaurant competition, a difficulty in hiring qualified people due to a tight labor market, an increase in food costs. Those were the ingredients, and it was a recipe for disaster. Sound familiar? It should – variations on this recipe are being served nationwide.

This is not the first time this has ever happened to anyone. And it won't be the last. People lose jobs all the time. It's a fact of life. The current fact of American business. There are the big stories. (See Enron, Tyco, Worldcom, and a variety of other companies too numerous to mention.) And there are the people-sized stories, too.

What about my familiy? How will we afford those braces Martha needs? How will Julie go to college? What about my weekly golf game? Who will pay for the Mercedes?

The Reality Check Shows Up

Wait a minute. I'm a senior executive. I'm a major shareholder. I start to dream again.... The sun was shining brightly....

"Steve…will you please wake up!"

Oops, it's Ralph. The sun sinks. It's over. I'm losing it!

"You're losing it! We're all losing it!" And with those immortal words – "we're all losing it!" – we lost it.

No fanfare, no parade, no trumpet blare. No news flash. Nothing! It just ended.

And even if I sort of saw it coming, nothing could prepare me for how I would feel.

The pain I felt was truly awesome. So was the empty feeling.

A successful career in business down the drain. There was a thud, like a wrecking ball barreling into the side of a building, only it was my stomach.

If I looked up, I could see the bottom of the barrel high above me. And that's how I began my remarkable journey through the seven stages of successful unemployment.

Losing a job is initially like an out-of-body experience. It only happens to the other guy. It never happens to you.

Maybe you think, "I'm too good to be fired. I'm a valuable asset to the corporation. They'll find other ways to make ends meet. Surely, they won't let *me* go?"

Or maybe you expected it.

After all, it's happening more and more.

The sad fact is no one is safe in today's business environment. And I mean no one.

Just ask the people at Worldcom, Arthur Andersen, Enron, to name just a few. Or any once high-flying dot.com company.

The process of becoming unemployed varies by person, but here's a typical scenario.

First, someone asks you to come into their office. It's seldom done in your own office... too personal.

They inform you that you no longer have a job. "Your position has been eliminated." "We are downsizing your department." "We are closing the facility." "My daughter is replacing you." The list of reasons is endless.

Next, you pack up your office belongings, in some instances, in the presence of a human resources person. You'll probably have to sign something, and that's it.

You might be entitled to a severance package that includes paychecks, health and 401(k) benefits, etc. Thus you still might actually be receiving money. That's great, but remember, the severance package will run out, and the reality of no income will surface again. Be prepared when this occurs.

The "U" Word

Unemployment. The most dreaded word in the English language. OK, maybe it's not, but it has to come close to the top of the most dreaded list. It tugs at your heart. It makes you an outcast from working society.

It lowers your self-esteem. You become the bottom figure of the totem pole of life. Or lower. At least that's the way it seems. And that's the way it feels.

Suddenly there's no need for you to put on a suit and tie or skirt and blouse and go to the office the next morning.

You've disappeared. When you call up and ask for messages, they answer, "Who's he?" In addition, your voice-mail box is eliminated, your e-mail address is deleted, and overnight or faster you've gone from "who's who" to "who's he?"

Remember when Jerry McGuire quits? The office stops for a moment, and then everyone goes back to work.

And the big one: no more paychecks. This is a sure sign that you've entered into the unemployment zone.

It reshapes your whole view of the world.

Forget Copernicus. Your world revolves around you.

If your neighbor is unemployed, it's a recession. If you're unemployed, it's a depression. I think I'm depressed.

I spent some time avoiding the "U word." It took awhile. I think I used up every other letter in the alphabet except U.

Ah, the reasoning. The company was "reorganizing." We were evaluating our survival in spite of, let me see, a large bank debt, a dwindling customer base, a reduced restaurant staff, and limited cash flow.

For me, it was one of those high-class things. I was the number-two executive, fired by my number one.

When it was done, I really felt like number two.

My First Full Day of Unemployment

There I was cleaning out my desk. Removing memorabilia, whatever that is, from every nook and cranny, whatever that is.

There goes my portrait of Colonel Sanders. (I used to work for him.) The Chinese calendar.

What year is it, anyway? The year of the Horse. Whoa.

For me it's the Year of the Glue Factory!

It's truly amazing how much garbage you can accumulate. And the even more amazing thing is that each piece is even more useless then the one before. Truly amazing.

In your office, there always seems to be a place for stuff like that. Now that I have to take it home I realize how useless it all really is. How much reality can a person handle?

Besides pictures of my family, what other useful items were in the office? Hmmm… the Chicago Bulls basketball hoop attached to the wastebasket – for those important memos.

The volumes of past memos and business documents that I kept from other companies, figuring that someday that old stuff would be valuable reference material.

All the more valuable because now there are at least ten layers of dust on that multilayered stack-o-memos. The fact is, I haven't looked at any of it in five years.

"Hey, I can't throw this out," you say to yourself. "I'm sure I'll need it tomorrow." The gag gift of a jockstrap with a Brillo pad attached to it. Very funny!

The Velcro dartboard and balls (maybe I'll need the balls) and all those executive decision-making devices that are really quite funny when you're an executive making decisions.

Hey, maybe your useless array of memorabilia is better than mine, but if you find yourself looking at boxes and boxes of junk, don't worry. It's just another day in the U-Zone.

And so it goes. From tropical daydreams to cold reality. From the beach house to the outhouse.

My First Full Day Continues...

I was angry at everyone, and I was depressed. How can this happen to me? I thought I was brilliant. And now I had the time to contemplate some of my not-so-brilliant decisions.

We'd been in the restaurant business. Restaurant customers, like other business customers, can be very fickle. If you don't meet their needs, they go other places.

We had to raise prices, we were forced to pick secondary locations for our unit development. Even when we were fully staffed, our staff was in constant turnover.

Even though we thought we had a viable strategic plan for growth, we didn't grow.

I had warnings about my impending doom, but I basically ignored them. I was from the "if you have a positive attitude and believe you can fix the problem, you can" school.

So I put all my efforts toward saving the business.

Sadly, in some cases, no matter how hard you try, it doesn't work and you become a victim of unemployment.

And, at that moment, I knew who to blame. Me.

Warning signs or not, any one of us can be caught up in the U-Zone. It was my turn. And it was weird.

I remember coming home that night.

"Honey, I'm Home"

Then there's the look-at-the-bright-side approach. "Hey, we have our health, the family is together, our relationship is stronger than ever, right?" "We'll manage, won't we?"

A tip. During this initial shock period, you might want to think twice before you ask a question that warrants an answer.

If you do ask a question, you better be ready for the answer.

Now, don't get me wrong. If you have a strong marriage or relationship, you will probably get through this time in your life just fine, as my wife and I did.

But don't be complacent about your relationship.

Being unemployed can (and will) put a heavy stress on even the strongest relationship. It's a reality of life.

There are thousands of families and relationships that fall apart because of unemployment.

Talk the situation over openly with your spouse. Say how you feel and explain that finding another opportunity might take some time. Let your spouse work out his or her feelings.

This is especially important if you have a spouse who has never been unemployed. My wife is a teacher. She never experienced unemployment. Her perspective of the job search process was different than mine.

Seek support from your family. Since members of your family will probably have to make some sacrifices, determine who has to make them and what they will be.

Again, an open dialog is crucial. Not easy, but crucial.

Work jointly to develop a budget. Money, or the lack thereof, may become an issue. Did I say may? Make that *will*.

If you're fortunate enough to receive a severance package, that's great, but remember, getting a job can be a long process.

Plan for the lack of funds accordingly, even if you're lucky enough to have a decent severance package.

Finally, create a contingency plan to cover the "what ifs."

These are those unexpected things that pop up when you least expect them. In other words, prepare for the worst.

No matter how long you've been married, no matter how strong your marriage is, when you come home to tell your wife or husband you're unemployed you're entering a time period that will definitely stress even the best relationship.

The shock of being unemployed is, in many cases, difficult to comprehend. If it has never happened to you before, it can be a terrrifying experience.

Even if you already experienced unemployment, it still has a devastating effect on your current life and behavior.

There you are, working at your job, doing all that's requested of you. You're paying attention to all the rumors floating around, but you're convinced you're safe.

That's common – most employees don't go around thinking they'll be laid off or fired.

Small signs appear, but you ignore them.

Some Advice I Wish I'd Had

When small danger signs begin to appear at work, pay attention. Although it might not alleviate your upcoming unemployment, if you can prepare for your possible unemployment and begin the job search process while you're still employed, stress levels can be reduced dramatically.

What are some of those danger signs? That varies by the size of the company or by industry or by job function.

First, overtime might be reduced, nonessential travel might be eliminated.

You might also notice some small projects being delayed and a deferment or reduction of scheduled pay increases.

The payment of bonuses (if earned) might be delayed.

Small capital improvements might not occur. More senior-level management meetings may be held after regular office hours.

These small danger signs can be a prelude to larger, more dramatic signals, such as a major reduction in all travel, a delay of vital projects, a reduction or elimination of training programs, marketing cutbacks, an increase in outsourcing, and the disappearance of outside contractors or consultants.

Overtime might be totally eliminated, or it might increase as companies try to get by without hiring. Sometimes it's hard to tell what's a warning sign. But if any of these signs start to occur in your work life, you can all too often be assured that something is happening – and it's probably not good.

If your organization brings in a consulting company to evaluate processes, analyze workflow, or reevaluate job descriptions and responsibilities, or if your organization considers a merger or other business consolidation, don't be fooled.

Something is occurring, and it could easily affect your position or department negatively.

A Quick Note for Those in the "Pre-U" Mode

You might want to be sure you have copies of the files you need. Even if you have some sort of "noncompete" clause, you're entitled to a copy of such things as a file of your business contacts and acquaintances.

The week before what was to be his last day, a friend of mine bought a box of discs and took home copies of possibly useful files. Or send yourself information via e-mail.

Print out a hard copy of your database. That way, you're not stuck if you no longer have the software.

Whatever you do, stop hallucinating. Stop thinking that unemployment can't happen to you, because it can. And if you're already unemployed, you might want to reflect on what those warning signs were in your work life.

Because, let's face it, in the working world to come, we'll all have to be a lot smarter – and maybe a little more suspicious.

By the way, hallucinating is also a trait of the unemployed.

You develop a strange sense of humor. This book for example. The humor emerges to fill in those empty spaces.

A man walks into a psychiatrist's office. He says, "Doctor for the past several weeks I feel that I'm invisible." The doctor says, "I'm sorry, I can't see you now."

A man is outside a fancy bar trying to get in to join his pals for a drink or two. The maître d' does not allow him to enter because the gentleman is not wearing a tie.

After several minutes of arguing and not getting in, the man leaves for his car. At his car he notices a pair of jumper cables. He places them around his neck, ties a nice knot, and goes back to join his friends at the restaurant.

As he walks in, the maître d' looks at him and says, "OK, I guess I'll have to let you in, but just don't start anything."

Don't ever lose your sense of humor.

"A funny thing happened on the way to the office this morning. It disappeared."

It's Still That First Night...

Dinner is served. Dinner is over.

It was quicker than most. Although it seemed like an eternity. No in-depth conversation to speak of at this point. Just a blank stare here and there.

The rest of the evening is spent watching television. More blank stares. Futile attempts at idle conversation. Or maybe idle attempts at futile conversation. I don't quite remember.

Bedtime isn't much better. There is a better than average probability your physical relationship will also become somewhat strained. You can tell things are a little strained when you come to bed, look over to the other side, and see nothing but back. It's a pretty strong hint that amorous thoughts will not turn into reality.

Oh, you can try and be romantic, but the odds of success are less than those of finding a job overnight.

"Goodnight, sweetheart." "See you in the morning."

How bad could it be? You think, "We've saved some money, and, hey, I have a rich uncle. If this takes longer than I expect, I can always hit him up for a couple of dollars."

Remember what I said about hallucinations?

"Fairy tales can come true, it can happen to you…"

You think. You dream.

"The sun was shining brightly on the small tropical isle…"

Zzzzzzzzzz.

"What's that? Is it morning already?"

The start of a new exciting day. I've got lots of things to do. You still have what I call "leftover thoughts."

You think, "We're still trying to get that financing package together." You remember full days. Lunch at the club. Racquetball at 6:00. Dinner with the investors.

And always… a busy day at the office.

You mean it wasn't a dream? I don't have to go in?

Of course I do. I'm a valuable member of the executive team…Not any more. And so it goes.

You're unemployed, stupid.

The reality of unemployment usually takes more than a day to comprehend. Sometimes you really do believe it was all a dream. That it can't happen to you.

But it can, especially in today's business environment. It's not something you accept readily.

It truly is a difficult concept to grasp.

In fact, you're not even at Stage One yet.

You're still playing "How Low Can You Go?"

Feeling sorry for yourself. In the corporate trash can.

Welcome to the U-Zone.

The U-Zone

Unhappy. Unfortunate. Unemployed. Don't forget ugly.

If you are unemployed, you are in the U-Zone.

The more you dwell on the negative, the harder it will be to regroup and search for that exciting new opportunity that will eventually come your way.

So here's a key to getting your head out of the U-Zone.

(By the way, it took me quite awhile to come up with a lot of this wonderful advice. It sure didn't happen during those first few days – while I was still stunned. It's pretty good advice, and you'll want to start using it as soon as you can.)

Use unemployment as a positive life experience and move ahead. The purpose of this book is to make a difficult period in your life a little less difficult, a little less stressful, and slightly more humorous.

Heck, you have extra time to read, let's make the most of it.

In some instances, since the initial feeling you get from being unemployed is like a death (the death of your company or job), it doesn't hurt for it to be handled in a similar manner.

Different religions and cultures have different ways to handle a death. Most of them rely on close socialization to get you through the experience.

My tip…allow yourself a one-week period to mourn.

If you want to pity yourself – and that's quite normal – do it during this seven-day period and then move on.

As best you can, try not to be embarrassed about your situation (in this economy, you've got a lot of company). Don't be afraid to use the support system of close friends and relatives to help you through this period.

I think it's sort of like sitting shivah or holding a wake, where after the death of a loved one, people visit you and each other to provide support, comfort, and bring a pile of food. This food will become helpful since you're now unemployed and money might become scarce.

Anyway, during this period, the purpose is to help your mind adjust to the death and loss that has occurred, and it allows you to move forward faster. If you allow a longer period than one week, it will envelop you and that is bad. Mourn. Do it deeply and truly.

Cry. Scream. Feel the pain of your loss.

Be angry. You're right, it's unfair.

How could they? After all you've done.

Get into it. And then... get over it.

Because it's time to get on with your life.

Oh, sure, for the first few days you might mope around the house feeling sorry for yourself and feel pathetic and believe that no one cares. That's normal. Who can blame you?

But you know the real feeling a lot of your friends have? They're sorry for you, but they're glad it wasn't them.

And if the situation was reversed, that's how you'd feel.

There's a lot of sad and negative stuff going on.

But the quicker you get the mourning period over, the sooner you can get started on finding that new opportunity.

And that opportunity will come. Maybe not soon.

And probably not easily. But it will come if you hang in there. So let's get with the program.

Years ago it was different. Back then you got a job. You performed it well, and twenty or thirty years later you retired to a house in the Hamptons, wherever that is, or Ft. Lauderdale or Lake Havasu City (I know where they are). Today, it's every person for him- or herself.

In many ways, loyalty to an employee has become a thing of the past. Sad but true. And it cuts both ways.

Loyalty to a job or an employer also seems to have become a thing of the past. Also sad. Also true.

Today loyalty is a concept practiced by fewer employers. Just look around. Or look in the mirror. It's happened to a lot of people lately.

Visit the unemployment office or watch a news report on television or read your local newspaper.

Unfortunately, it's a trend. There's a bit of good news here – you're not alone. In fact, it has happened to so many that the shame of the "Scarlet U" is less than it used to be.

So now it's time to cope. How do you function during the dreaded period of unemployment?

That's what this book is all about. It's a how-to book to get you motivated and provide you with the tools you'll need to find that new opportunity. And it lets you know you're not alone and that conditions will improve.

I'm not a psychologist, but I can offer you some insight from an individual who has been there, gone through it, and with hard work, support of family and friends, and working through the "Seven Stages" turned this difficult part of my life into a positive, life-altering experience.

Warning: Don't StayStuck in the U-Zone

Going through unemployment and coming out the other side (i.e., employed) is a series of stages. I counted seven of 'em.

You'll have to work through them. Usually, one at a time.

Right now, we're still sort of pre-Stage One.

You're dealing with the idea that you're unemployed.

On some levels, this is a pretty easy concept to grasp.

Here is a simple rule to follow: No job or paycheck… unemployed. Have a job and a paycheck… employed.

In actuality, it is a bit more complicated than this.

If you're not careful, you'll end up stuck in the U-Zone. "Successful" unemployment demands that you get past that.

You'll need to move out of the U-Zone and start moving through your own seven stages of successful unemployment.

It's not rocket science, as they say, but it is a lot of hard work – and there are tough times ahead.

To help you get ready, here's a sneak preview!

The Seven Stages – A Sneak Preview
Stage One… Putting Up a Positive Front

You're still going to have a lot of emotions – a lot of emotions – but you need to wake up and smell the ugly fact. Turn your emotions into something positive and start to develop a plan.

This is easier said than done. In many instances, when a person loses a job, they just don't want to admit it.

You have to do more than admit it. You have to come to terms with unemployment quickly, embrace the fact, and begin moving forward. You now know you're unemployed, your usefulness to the company is gone, and they have decided "to move in another direction."

Losing one's effectiveness is tough to accept, but you have to remember, it happens all the time. You're not alone.

Let's look at sports. How many times have you read about team managers or coaches being fired because they couldn't win with what they had ("they're ineffective").

Often, within a short period of time, they get hired by another team. It's the same in business, turnover is a constant. People are always being fired, downsized, or removed from their positions.

So even if one company put you in the "out box" for whatever reason, I guarantee you there is another company that will think you're just what they're looking for. The key is finding that company. That's where the Seven Stages come into play.

The next chapter will help you get through that acceptance stage. Once that is accomplished you will be able to move on to developing a résumé.

Stage Two...
Accepting the Fact You're Unemployed

Unlike Stage One, which is easily identifiable, this stage is a little more difficult. Oh sure, you can consciously say, "I'm no longer employed," but accepting it in the old unconscious – sorry, that's subconscious – is slightly more difficult.

Facing up to the fact may cause you to adopt a low opinion of yourself, so it's natural that you may try to avoid the issue by thinking of things you'd do at the office, if you had an office.

Acceptance, however, is a critical stage.

In order to move to Stage Three, you must accept the fact of you're unemployment. It's sort of like acquiring a possibly fatal disease. You must accept the fact that you have it, and do what is necessary to cure it.

So, how do you come to accept this fact? In my experience, you have to do some mental and emotional judo – you have to find a way to turn it into a positive situation.

This is not an easy concept to grasp, but it can lead to sanity, lower blood pressure, and an adventure you thought you'd never undertake.

Hey, maybe it's an adventure you don't want to undertake. But since there's no alternative, go for it!

Strategy one is to avoid sitting around the house and feeling sorry for yourself. This can be detrimental to your health as well as to your prospecting.

Accepting the fact that you're unemployed means you can move to the next stage.

Without this acceptance, you will remain in a state of suspended animation and reenter the dreaded U-Zone.

Time, furthermore, does not stand still. Neither do expenses.

Accepting unemployment means understanding a few things:

- **First, you're not alone.**
- **Second, you're not an outcast.**
- **Finally, you're not a failure.**

Unlucky? Maybe. Successful? Not just now.

But just like the flu, it's something that can happen to anyone. And, like the flu, you can get over it.

In fact, as you progress and succeed in the business world you may realize that the more successful you are, the greater the chance that sooner or later you will become unemployed. Hey, even Jack Welch has faced unemployment.

Naturally this is more prevalent if you work for someone else than if you're self-employed. Not many people fire themselves.

But you can lose your business, which has a similar result.

Accepting the fact of unemployment means you can now move on to finding that new opportunity.

You will find that new opportunity. You might not believe it now, but you will later.

A quote I found very inspiring during my unemployment was "If you can see it and you can believe it, you can achieve it." So imagine your new career, believe in yourself, work toward your goal, and you will achieve employment.

Stage Three... Developing the Résumé

A résumé is a short account of your career and qualifications. In many ways, it's a stroll down memory lane as seen through rose-colored glasses.

There is a saying that "everyone looks good on their résumé." I've seen enough résumés to know that if many people lived up to their résumé, they could probably be president – not of a company, but the country.

Based on the job the current administration is doing as I'm finishing this book, it wouldn't be hard to qualify. Hey, maybe I'll send in my résumé.

The administration I'm talking about as I write this book might be different than the administration in office when you read this book. But job loss and economic dislocation is a part of every administration – because it's a part of our modern economy.

There are hundreds of ways to develop a résumé.

Make sure that when you develop yours, it is targeted for the specific assignment you're seeking.

For those searching in a number of directions, it is not uncommon to have a number of different résumés.

The rule of thumb is to make sure that your résumé reflects your strategy for finding a new career opportunity. We'll talk about creating your résumé in a later chapter.

Stage Four...
Getting Your Unemployment Benefits

Today, a lot of benefit work can be done online or over the telephone, but you still have to apply. Depending on your experience level, this could be the toughest stage. It's one thing to put up a positive front, it's another to accept it, but it's something quite different to admit it in public.

And it may not be a pleasant experience. Wait in this line. Fill out this form. Go to this meeting. Meet with this counselor. Come back in a week. Come back in two weeks.

Now stand in this line. Wait here. List those job contacts.

This is embarrassing. I don't want to do this.

There has to be a better way. Maybe?

But not if you want to receive some money.

You may feel slightly guilty and reluctant to file for unemployment benefits. Well, *snap out of it!*

It's your right as a citizen. They owe you.

Don't feel embarrassed. If anyone should feel guilty or embarrassed, it should be our government employees and our politicians. After all, they've been accepting money doing nothing for years. Just go down to the office and do what they want.

The benefit amount isn't much, but it does help your mental attitude, and it is a "paycheck." We'll be discussing the intricacies of filing for compensation a bit later, so be patient.

Stage Five... Creating a Plan

OK, you've put up a positive front. You've even accepted it. You've developed your résumé, and you've gone down to the unemployment office. Now comes the next stage...figuring out a way to find a job. And you have to do it with that social problem known as...unemployment breath!

Believe it. You've got a better chance of finding water in the Sahara, or Bigfoot, or the Loch Ness monster than you do of getting a job immediately. Regardless of the type of job you're looking for, you'll need realistic goals.

The old saying was to give yourself a month for every $10,000 in salary you expect to earn. I think it's probably longer than that, particularly in today's environment.

Whatever the timetable you set up for yourself, be realistic. Ensure you take into account the industry dynamics (it might take longer to find a job in high-tech or telecommunications), the position you're searching for (there aren't as many senior-level positions as there once were so it might take more time to find one), your salary requirements (the higher the salary, the longer it takes), your location requirements (if you can't move, allow more time to find a job), etc.

Developing a strategy with a realistic timetable can make your life a little more palatable. And more importantly, it will ease some of the potential family tension. If everyone knows what a realistic timetable is, some of the family stress might disappear. Not all of it, but some.

If your wife or husband is not in business, she or he will probably be all over you to get a job, quickly.

Your spouse may not understand a long timetable, but at least he or she will be included in the decision loop, eliminating some stress. And eliminating stress makes job interviewing and life easier.

One other point. To the best of your ability, don't be embarrassed about your situation. Don't get me wrong, I wouldn't take out an ad in the newspaper publicizing your situation, but I wouldn't avoid it either.

Like death, the "U word" is not easily discussed. People who are employed feel terrible about talking to people who aren't and vice versa. There are a lot of reasons for this – some real, some superstitious. For example, a surprising number of people are worried it might be contagious.

Stage Six...Making It Happen

This means getting off your butt to start making the necessary contacts to be successful. Remember, a lot of people have been unemployed at least once in their career.

It may mean contacting just about every person you've ever met. Old friends, new friends, old business acquaintances, neighbors, church members, bowling buddies, etc.

There is almost no limit to this. No one is off limits. And I mean no one.

"Hello, Fred. Yea, it's Steve. Steve Zipkoff. You remember. We were friends in grammar school. What's it been, thirty years? Long time no see. Oh, I haven't lived there in twenty-two years. How's the family? Great. So Fred, I was wondering. Are you still selling Edsels?"

It might be a little awkward, but every contact counts.
Some day Fred might be contacting you.
By the way, Stage Six might take a while. Be prepared.

Stage Seven... Hallelujah!

Eventually, you will have what Oprah Winfrey calls a "hallelujah moment!" You will have found a new job.

It will happen. No one can say when it will happen, but it will happen. The right job, the right city, the right money. Well, maybe two out of three.

A great new job. Where have you been all my life? Why didn't I find you months ago...years ago? This is the greatest thing that has ever happened to me. Cue the music. "Is this really a job offer? Is it really there? Is this a mirage?"

For you and your spouse it has not been a honeymoon suite. Things have probably been a little tense. Well, no more.

It's true. You have a job. It pays. A real paycheck! Perhaps you'd like to frame it, but you need the money.

One good thing about pain, maybe the only thing, is that once it's over, you don't remember what it feels like. Though some trauma remains, the human mind does not like to dwell on the negative. You can remember you had a feeling you don't want to experience again, but the intricate detail of pain vanishes.

The emotional roller coaster ride is over. And now the moment you've been waiting for.

OK, end of sneak preview.
Time to take it from the top – or the bottom.

We will now go into intimate detail of each stage as we maneuver through the exciting mine fields of unemployment. Please fasten your seat belt.

Place the mask over your nose and mouth first.

This ride can be dangerous, but it will be rewarding.

Here we go…from Hell to Hallelujah!

Stage One... Putting up a Positive Front

"He who walks with the wise grows wise."

The Daydream to Reality

The American Dream consists of working. We have been taught to put in our nine to five, or longer. When you no longer function in this realm, you and society consider yourself a failure, a has-been, perhaps a never-was, a person no longer valuable to society. This might have been true in the past, but it is no longer true today.

Just look around. How many people do you know or read about who are unemployed? The numbers are startling.

Much of today's business environment is not employee oriented. It is employer and shareholder driven. Now, don't get me wrong – companies must make money and provide investors a decent return on investment, otherwise the business cannot survive. But employees still must be considered a valuable asset, and that appears to be changing.

Many of you may have investments in a variety of businesses, either through your own investing, your 401(k) plans, or through a number of pension funds. How a company performs is crucial for your own portfolio growth.

But have you ever noticed what usually happens to a stock price when a company announces a reorganization and a coinciding reduction in staff?

The stock price usually increases.

That means investors (Wall Street) view staff layoffs as a good thing. Then again, when unemployment figures reach high numbers, that's a bad thing. I still haven't been able to figure that out, even though I'm an investor, too.

Problems and Opportunities

Where was I…yes, unemployment. Once unemployment hits, it normally has a snowball effect.

It usually doesn't stop with one or two people. It can affect an entire organization, a department, a division, etc.

This is where your ability to read signs can be very helpful. Just being able to anticipate problems can open up opportunities. If you're in tune to what's going on in your company, you can get a pretty good idea as to what's coming. I mentioned earlier that small danger signs can lead to more dramatic signals. Pay attention to them and determine your best course of action.

Putting up a positive front means you pay attention to your surroundings, you analyze the situation, you determine a course of action, and you develop a plan to move forward.

Most companies have certain ways of doing things. Policies and procedures are in place to handle various work situations. Work processes are in effect to ensure things "get done our way." If things begin to change, if work functions are altered, if processes are modified…those are signs that something is happening that might affect employment.

If quarterly results do not live up to expectations or forecasts, that is a signal that some change might be in the air.

Don't ignore these indicators.

It may be hazardous to your job.

Remember Jeff Foxworthy's routine, "You might be a redneck…if?" Well, the same holds true for unemployment. When you analyze the situation, it is important to place yourself at the top of the priority list. Determine how changes will affect what you're doing within the organization. For example, if you're in the marketing department and the last several marketing campaigns have been failures, there is a real good chance you might be heading for unemployment.

If you're in the accounting department and a new accounting software package is purchased in order to reduce the employee workload and speed up certain processes to "save the company money," you might be heading for unemployment.

If you're in sales and overall revenue has slipped to a precarious level because no new deals have closed lately, you might be heading for unemployment.

If you're in a development department and it is decided that there will not be any development because money is tight, you might be heading for unemployment.

The list is almost endless. Maybe not funny, but endless.

Once signs occur, it is crucial to determine a course of action. This will provide you with the tools necessary to move forward. When individuals are confronted with negative situations they must determine what to do.

Now pay attention, I think this is great.

Understanding problems ahead of time is one of the first (and best) ways to identify the opportunity.

But let's say you're already in the U-Zone.

How to Move Forward, Positively

There are several ways to approach your problem. You can (1) look at the negative situation and treat it negatively – this usually means depression, suffering, and staying stuck in the U-Zone; (2) look at the situation ambivalently, meaning "I can go either way, it doesn't matter"; or (3) seize the moment, grasp the situation by the horns, and treat it as an experience with potential positives.

For a start, you're going to learn from it.

Sometimes we don't have a lot of choices.

This is one of those times.

Your only real alternative is to seize the moment, grasp this unhappy situation by the horns, and turn it around.

Make the decision to treat it as a positive experience.

Is this hard to accomplish? Yes, it is. But it is your only real alternative. First, it motivates you to action.

How can you take a negative like unemployment and turn it into a positive? First, by adopting a positive mental attitude. That means believing in yourself. It also means going out every day and working to make it happen. It means keeping at it until you find an opportunity that fits.

Don't look at it as unemployment. You've got a job. You're now employed in search of another business opportunity.

After all, most companies are searching for new business they would like you to work on.

So if you're unemployed, you're at a point where you're searching for new business.

If you're unemployed, think of yourself as searching for a client who has a piece of business they'd like you to work on.

In today's business environment, being unemployed is no longer the stigma it once was. It's almost the rule rather than the exception. Just look at the statistics. Almost everyone at one point in time or another has been unemployed. And if they haven't been, just wait…they will.

So start looking for positives. The key to finding a new business opportunity is simply that. Finding it.

FindIng Your Opportunity Is #1

Looking for opportunity is an initial positive action step that will guide you towards reemployment.

We'll talk about the plan in a later stage.

Suffice it to say, a positive mental attitude is paramount to moving toward that new position.

One important fact to realize is that when you're looking for a new opportunity, it is your number-one priority, and it must be, but it will be no one else's number-one priority, except your family's.

This is very important to understand and accept. It doesn't mean that people are rude, although some people are. And it doesn't mean they don't care, although some people don't. It just means you're low on their *to do* list.

Think of your own business situation, when you had a job.

You had tons of things to do. Meeting people who weren't part of your normal business environment and returning calls were usually low on the priority list, especially if your boss was always on your case to complete that critical assignment.

For example, if you're meeting a person and trying to determine whether an opportunity is available, understand that the person talking with you has many other priorities on his or her mind. Each priority is more important than you.

If he has eight priorities, you will be number nine. If he has ten priorities, you will be number eleven. If he has one hundred priorities, don't talk to him. He's probably crazy and is in the process of becoming unemployed, too.

There's one exception to this general rule – when that person has a job they need to fill *right away*.

Suddenly, their problem can become your opportunity.

Remember, companies have been downsizing for quite some time. Everyone is running lean. A person leaving a new project can instantly put an overstretched company into crisis mode.

That's when the positive vibes you've been putting out can really pay off. If they like you (instead of pity you), if they feel you'd be a good person to add to the team – well, it's just amazing how fast it can happen. And you never know when.

Don't expect your phone to ring off the wall, either. (This, of course, is even less likely if your phone isn't mounted on the wall in the first place.)

Don't expect a lot of return phone calls.

But don't stop being *pleasantly* persistent.

If you've kept it positive, you might be the one they call when that job suddenly opens up.

"Fortune favors the prepared mind," and "an opportunity and an unprepared man equal a fool." That means you must take the initiative. You must make the phone calls.

You must return the calls. You must go out of your way to be available at their convenience, not yours. You must do the apologizing when you show up for a meeting and the person you were to meet is out of town and forgot to reschedule the meeting. It all falls into your responsibility. Remember, you're the person looking for the opportunity, not the person you're meeting. Maybe someday the shoe will be on the other foot, but not today. Today is your turn to be humble.

I recently went back to my files to see how many people I met during my initial stage of setting up a network. (This stage will be discussed later.) I was amazed at the number.

I was even more astonished at the names and their positions. I can tell you this, if I was not searching for another opportunity, I would never have been in contact with so many highly placed company officers.

If I just went along and performed my job as most of us do, I never would have met all these people. That would have been a great loss, since later on in my career they became instrumental contacts in growing my own business.

So being unemployed really can be a positive situation. And when you do finally find that really new opportunity, you will have all these business contacts to use for mentoring, sounding boards, raising capital, etc.

When You're Smiling...

Working to put up a positive front will also put you in a positive frame of mind. And believe me, a lot of times, if you don't have that, you don't have anything.

Maintaining that attitude is important because your attitude is easily identifiable when you're setting up a job network or interviewing for a new opportunity.

If it comes across that your frame of mind is less than positive, it will affect every meeting you have. Although you may be able to concentrate, the people you're meeting will automatically set up a barrier and tune you out. You will not receive the assistance you need, and more importantly, you will be perceived as a negative person. Add that to your current state of unemployment and you've got a double negative, and a double negative does not make a positive.

So be positive. Smile as much as you can. Talk about your situation with energy and realistic enthusiasm! Don't let people see you in a negative mood. When in public, always – I repeat – always **have a positive attitude**.

Remember, people try to avoid negative situations. They do everything in their power to keep away from them. Being unemployed is a negative situation, thus you will be avoided. Not on purpose, but it will happen.

By the way, the minute you do find a new opportunity, it will be like a new flower blossoming. Your friends will come out of the woodwork and exclaim, "Where have you been? We've missed you."

However, if people know you're unemployed and see you in a positive light, they will adopt a positive attitude towards you. They'll say, "I wish I could handle adversity as well as Steve." (By the way, if your name isn't Steve, fill in your own name here.) "If he is like that when he's unemployed, just imagine what he'd be like when things are going well. He's the kind of guy I'll do everything I can to help." "I'll find an opportunity for him. What a guy."

So put up that positive front. And keep it up. You're going to have to learn to make the most of a negative situation.

Once you've put up a positive front, you can now move on to what I consider to be the hardest part of the unemployment picture – accepting the fact you're unemployed.

Stage Two...
Accepting the Fact

Even an unemployed person needs management skills – and right now your main management responsibility is you. Though, you might need a bit of help.

Sharing Can Help

OK, so now you're positive, but you're still depressed as ever. And even if you're maintaining that positive exterior, the interior needs a little work.

In *some* instances, your spouse won't talk to you, or she or he is now bringing up things that have irritated her or him for years. Maybe there's no paycheck – but it's payback time.

Understand that being unemployed can strain a relationship. Be prepared. Discuss your situation and feelings as openly as possible and ask for understanding and guidance. Speaking of guidance, you might try some low-cost counseling. Working together can be an important step toward accepting the fact that you're unemployed. Counseling can also help you develop effective employment strategies.

Unemployment is not a situation you should handle yourself. If you have a support system (family or friends), they can play a major role in helping you move forward. Utilize support systems whenever possible.

Support systems make coping with unemployment easier and provide the people affected by your unemployment an understanding of the process you will be going through to find that new opportunity.

Communicating with family and friends will reduce their stress level and thus provide a forum for positive thoughts and actions.

During my period of unemployment, I was constantly updating my family on my progress. I had my wife review my résumé. I kept my children updated on generalities of my progress. (Depending on the ages of your children and their capacity to understand the situation, you might not want to do this. That is up to you and your circumstances.)My wife and I have been married for more than thirty-six years, and even though our relationship was solid, unemployment can have a negative impact on any relationship. We made it. We don't look back on that period fondly – though I love her more than ever for her support during that tough time. I suggest an open line of communication be set up so no surprises occur as you search out that new opportunity.

Although unemployment does not necessarily lead to hard times and divorce, it can. Unemployment will put a major strain on any relationship, no matter how strong it is.

Accepting the fact that you're unemployed seems like an easy enough concept to comprehend. You wake up, you don't go to the office or your place of work, and you don't receive a paycheck. How hard is that to comprehend?

Accepting the fact that you're unemployed means that you must accept something that is very negative, something that you may never have encountered before.

For many (I was one of them), it became very difficult to accept. Denial (and I don't mean the river in Africa) is the mainstream of your thought process.

"This can't be happening to me?" Maybe I admitted the fact, but my ego was still reluctant to accept it.

Unemployment Training

But as mentioned earlier, no one is protected from unemployment's clutches. It is everywhere, regardless of where you live, what you do, what your social status is or how much money you earn. As a matter of fact, unemployment is so rampant I wonder if there should be college courses on the subject. Colleges could make a lot of tuition money by offering these types of courses.

I can see the Executive Development College catalog now…

UNEMPLOYMENT 101
Introduction to Unemployment

Learn the intricacies of being a nonappreciated employee.

Fundamentals of Getting Fired covers upsetting your boss and alienating all those around you.

New Directives in Downsizing explores how even though you're a high-performance employee, you can still be let go.

This three-credit course will teach you the various means of becoming unemployed – one of America's growth industries.

Learn the difference between being fired, laid off, downsized, and rightsized.

Learn how the subtle differences in reengineering, retooling, and/or restructuring still mean only one thing… unemployment.

Includes some "hands-on" laboratory work. No prerequisite coursework needed.

Monday – Wednesday – Friday, 9a.m. – 10a.m.

Since you're not working this is a good time. What else are you doing in the morning? Hey, at least it will get you up.

UNEMPLOYMENT 206
Unemployment & Recreation

This course will focus on the ability to search for a new position while undertaking recreational activities like golf, bowling, fishing, etc.

You will learn the rules and regulations of recreational activities while at the same time become proficient in making excuses for why you were not available for calls. Optional extra credit: suntan management skills assessment workshop.

For those students not normally exposed to the sun, a bottle of sunblock is provided. We recommend SPF 45.

This is an individualized course which students may finish early, but why would you want to? It is not necessary to have previous experience in the rules of the games.

Times and days to be announced. Must have your own equipment. A cell phone would also be a plus in case you get calls for job interviews while participating in these recreational activities.

But it is not required – if you don't have one, just bring a note from your voice mail.

UNEMPLOYMENT 225
The Government & the Unemployed

This course is offered in cooperation with the Employment Commission. Learn how to fill out government forms while at the same time receiving benefits.

Receive actual experience in dealing with inefficient, undereducated, noncaring government employees (they have jobs and could care less whether you have one or not).

Rudeness optional.

As an added bonus, learn how to be a government employee yourself so you can have a job until retirement without the fear of unemployment.

There will be a slight additional fee for this part of the course. Field trips include taking the postal exam.

Tuesday & Thursday, 10a.m. – Noon
Laboratory – Wednesday, 1p.m. – 3p.m.

UNEMPLOYMENT 352
The History of Unemployment

Learn about all the people through history who didn't have jobs and didn't do anything.

Tuesday, 11a.m. – Noon. Lunch included in fees.

UNEMPLOYMENT 369
How to Search for and Catch a Rich Spouse

Not recommended for the married person (unless you have a note from your current spouse), this unique course will use rare film footage to explore *How to Marry a Millionaire*.

You will learn how some of the greatest gold diggers identify, pursue, catch, and marry wealthy individuals.

Learn the intricacies of entrapment and strategies to avoid a long jail sentence if some laws are broken.

Explore techniques of such famous personalities as Zsa Zsa Gabor, Marla Maples, Anna Nicole Smith, etc.

Successful completion of this course ensures you will not have to work again, thus avoiding the state of unemployment.

Friday & Saturday, 10p.m. till closing, various bars and party houses. There is an additional $3,000 fee for this course.

A deferred payment plan is available through the financial aid office contingent upon a successful marriage.

Low student loan interest rates are available.

Reality TV show in development.

UNEMPLOYMENT 469
Earning a Living While Remaining Unemployed

This graduate course explores the particulars of consulting, guest lecturing, and authoring a book on the successful stages of unemployment.

Through the experiences of various guest presenters you will become proficient in making excuses why you're not employed, learn how to charge exorbitant fees for discussing your experiences, and, most importantly, how to write a book about being unemployed.

Friday 1p.m. – 3p.m.

Anyone interested in signing up for these courses can inquire within or e-mail us at ineedajob@who'skiddingwho.edu.

It's All More Normal Than You Think

Understand that the concept and state of unemployment is not new. It has happened to millions of people, and it will happen to millions more.

Eventually, it will happen to almost everyone. So lighten up a little. It's not so bad.

It's not like losing a lung or getting audited by the IRS. Well, maybe the latter. After all, you have two lungs.

So you look at the bright side. You have no job responsibilities for which you're evaluated. You can come and go as you please, assuming you have a place to come and go to.

You'll have the time to do all those "little things" you haven't had the time to do, like painting the house, fixing the fence, redoing the plumbing, calling the plumber to fix what you fixed, etc. Each day becomes a "honeydew" weekend. "Honey do this, and honey do that." Don't even think about saying, "I haven't got the time."

And if you're lucky enough to get a severance package, well then, you're getting paid for doing nothing.

Life is great, a paid vacation.

If you're not getting a severance package, well, at least there's unemployment compensation.

Coming soon to a chapter near you we'll discuss how you will spend this plethora of bucks. After you make the house payment, pay utility bills, gas up the car, and splurge on a value meal (sorry, no supersize). The good news – your government certainly knows how to provide for its taxpaying citizens. Just glad to be an American.

Oh yes… accepting the fact that you're unemployed.

Because you will view unemployment as a very negative experience (we went over this earlier), you will find it difficult to accept the circumstance of unemployment.

It's not exactly like a death, but in some people's minds, especially your spouse's, it's close.

Society has convinced most of us that having a job is acceptable and "normal" behavior (though a friend is having trouble convincing his twenty-two-year-old son). Thus not having a job is unacceptable and abnormal. So how do you go about accepting something that is not acceptable?

In my case, I took the unemployment time of my life and used it as a time to reflect on what I had been doing and where I wanted to go.

In other words, I asked myself the question, "What do I want to do when I grow up?"

This is not an easy question to answer. It means you have to do a whole lot of internal reflection to decide if it makes sense to continue to do what you've been doing.

It also means asking if you *want* to continue to do it. Or if you want to do something else, are you prepared to do it and take a risk of failure. "Wait a minute. Why worry about that," you say to yourself – you're already a failure.

These seem to be pit stops on the road to acceptance. It's a time to ask questions you thought you were too busy to ask. To look at options you may have never considered. And, along the way, doing all this thinking about this and that, you'll find you're beginning to accept the fact of your unemployment.

Traits of Successful People

People who are successful take risks. Ask any successful entrepreneur or businessman and I'll bet you their first business venture was not successful.

In more cases than not, they failed numerous times and were probably unemployed a number of times before they became successful.

In my own case, after doing my own self-analysis, I realized that working for major corporations was not what I wanted to do, and after taking the risk of starting my own business and accepting the fact that unemployment was not a stigma on my career, my business began to flourish.

At the time of this writing, that business is thirteen years old. I still get excited about coming to work everyday.

In fact, I don't consider it work, I consider it an adventure.

What you also need to know is that when I decided to start my own business, I had two children in college, all the expenses that go along with that, and a wife who was a teacher, so you know right off the bat, household income was not at a high level.

However, I learned very quickly that:
1. fear is a great motivator;
2. enthusiasm is critical for success;
3. a positive attitude can move mountains and is contagious; and
4. persistence can get you clients even when they tell you that you can't help them.

In other words, a no today doesn't mean no tomorrow.

You can take these four traits and apply them to anything you do in life, including searching for a new career opportunity. So let's go over those four traits one by one.

Fear Is a Great Motivator

When things get really bad and it looks like there is no where to go, fear kicks in. How you handle fear determines success or failure. When fear raised its ugly head for me, I decided to ignore the fear, and it motivated me. Instead of saying, "If I don't get a client today, I'm ruined," I said, "Today is the day I'm getting that client, and I will convince them that yes is the appropriate response."

Even if you just think like this, positive things begin to happen. In a job interview, if you show fear by thinking, "If I don't get this job, I don't know how I'll get by," you probably won't get that job.

Interviewers can smell fear. If they are onto it, they think you're probably not the right person for the job. Your chance of getting hired in that company is lost.

Companies don't like to hire people who are afraid, so keep fear abated.

Enthusiasm Is Critical for Success

If there are two people in a room and one is enthusiastic and one is not, who is noticed? Enthusiasm can be caught.

If you have it, you can easily infect others, and that is good. Company interviewers love to visit with enthusiastic people. If you're enthusiastic about a job position, or even about the company you just left, your positive attitude gets noticed.

Even if you have been without a job for a number of months, be enthusiastic about your circumstances.

Let people experience that enthusiasm and provide them with a reason to be positive about your experience.

That's when positive things occur.

A Positive Attitude

A positive attitude can affect you in two powerful ways:

    1. it can move mountains; and

    2. it's contagious.

So always remain positive. Do it enough on the outside, and it starts to happen on the inside.

If you talk to successful sales people (and getting a job is a sales situation), one of the most important traits they name when discussing their success is "having a positive attitude."

I remember a sales situation that recently happened to my wife and I. We were on vacation in Hawaii and wanted to take a helicopter tour of the Big Island. It was very expensive.

A person informed us that if we attended a timeshare presentation, that would knock 50% off the price of the tour.

We thought, "Hey, what the heck, we'll see it for an hour and save a ton of money."

It was a one-on-one sales pitch, and the salesman was so good and had such a positive attitude we almost bought the timeshare. However, sanity prevailed, and we said no.

That's when the salesman shook my hand and said in an extremely positive way, "Thank you for your help."

I looked at him quizzically and said, "Wait a minute. We said no. Why are you thanking us?"

He said, "I know you said no, but our research shows that for every no we get we are 33% closer to getting a yes, so you just got me one-third closer to a sale and a nice commission check!" Talk about a positive attitude. I have never forgotten that, and today I use that attitude each time I get a no.

When searching for a new opportunity, remember that for each no you get, you're getting closer to a yes.

Persistence

Persistence can get you:
1. clients; and
2. a new opportunity.

As mentioned earlier, a no today is not a no tomorrow. Most of my clients have told me the reason they became clients was my persistence.

That doesn't mean be a nag, it means stay on top of the situation and be prepared to follow up in a reasonable time period.

For example, if a potential client says, "It's not the right time." I'll give them three months and call again to see if now is the right time.

It's no different while looking for a new opportunity.

During your networking process (this will be discussed in a later stage), you might come across a company that doesn't have an opportunity but you find it an interesting organization.

Call them back in three months to see if the situation has changed. Even if you have taken another job because of necessity, don't be afraid to keep searching for the "perfect opportunity."

If you've interviewed with a company and were not hired, it still doesn't mean there is not an opportunity in the future. Today's business environment is so fluid that positions and opportunities are always surfacing.

One department in a company might be firing, another department in the same company might be hiring. Keeping abreast of the marketplace and applying persistence can distinguish you from other candidates and get you the opportunity you're looking for.

And remember, people who are successful in today's business environment as well as the world take negatives and make them positives. You read about them all the time.

For example, Joanna Barnes of Altoona, Pennsylvania, tripped down a flight of stairs and was heading for certain disaster. She managed to survive the fall and came up with the idea of rubber stairs. Today Joanna lives in a rubber room in Newark, New Jersey, collecting thousands of dollars a day for her invention. She took a negative and made it into a positive. Hey, I didn't say the example was any good, did I?

Get Ready

You can look down the fear path and feel afraid, or you can look down the opportunity path and feel motivated. Choose your path. So instead of looking at life through negative eyes, begin looking for positives and accept the fact that the road of life is filled with little detours. Go around them.

You must control your own destiny and make things go your way. There's an old saying, and it goes like this: "If you want your prayers answered, get off your knees."

If people keep telling you no, you're asking the wrong question or talking to the wrong people.
If people keep telling you it can't be done, find other people who will tell you it can be done. If you run into a brick wall, bounce off of it and run into it again and again and again.

Eventually you will find a weakness, and the wall will fall, or you will begin to look for another wall. Either way, you will be finding other opportunities and alternatives.

But this is definitely when the going gets tough and the tough get going. So polish up that cliché collection. Tighten that belt, cinch up that holster, batten down the hatches, don't take no for an answer, don't chew with your mouth open, etc., etc., etc. Now is when all of those clichés will come in handy.

Remember, the early bird gets the worm. But the second mouse gets the cheese.

Outline a strategy for your attack. You will only be able to do that once you've accepted the fact that you're unemployed and that it isn't that bad. Once you accept the fact that you're unemployed, courage will return. You will be able to start to take control of your life again. This, of course, assumes that you had control of it in the first place.

I keep saying that unemployment isn't that bad, and I really mean it. Every time I think things are pretty bad, I look around me and realize that they aren't. Being healthy and having a solid family structure are truly important.

Hopefully, you're healthy and you a have a solid family structure, too.

OK, so you might have to take money out of the bank or your retirement accounts, and you might have to cut back on certain things you normally do, like eating, but believe me, money can be replenished. It might take time, but it can be replenished if you acquire the traits we talked about earlier. Also, no matter how bleak things become, before you know it, positive things begin to happen. It's one of those forces of nature. You have to make sure you notice the positives where and when they occur.

As you can see, accepting the fact that you're unemployed is a difficult concept to grasp, but once you do accept it, you can move on to the next stage on your journey, developing your résumé.

Stage Three...
Developing the Résumé

"To build a great organization, you must hire people—not résumés."

Résumés Are Critical

There are hundreds of books on the market to explain how to develop a résumé. Ever wondered why?

That's because there are hundreds of opinions on how to develop one. A résumé should be developed based upon what you, as an opportunity seeker, think is right for you.

One résumé does not fit all. It's not like a pair of socks.

Some people think you must condense a résumé to one page.

Others think a résumé should be no longer than two pages.

Still others think a résumé should be as long as necessary to convey all of your business facts and accomplishments.

The résumé debate will last a long time without any definitive answer. In fact, it will probably never end.

A résumé isn't a mysterious document. It is simply a means for you to resume your career.

No matter what you've done in your business career you should always have an updated résumé available, especially when searching for a new opportunity.

You might call it a bio or a profile or a personal information sheet, but we know what it is, don't we?

If you don't have a résumé, begin to develop one.

There are excellent résumé formats available for free on the Internet. Simply search via Google or other search engines using keywords such as résumé writing, formats, outlines, etc. These formats are transferrable to an e-mail account, making them easy to send out to prospective employers.

If you currently have a résumé, create a better one, and if you think your résumé is the best it can be, make hundreds of copies.

If you believe you need help in creating a résumé, you can:
1. purchase one of hundreds of books on the subject;
2. go to a library and select one of the books about developing a résumé; or
3. ask a friend or business associate who you think is successful and might be able to provide guidance.

If you know a person in human resources who has been involved in the interview process and has seen a lot of résumés, ask him or her for assistance.

Whatever way you proceed, make certain your résumé is an accurate account of your business experience.

Although this is not a book on résumé development, I think it is my clear duty to provide you with my opinion on résumé development. I do this for the following reasons:
1. I've seen quite a number of résumés when I interviewed people for positions.
2. I've participated in the opportunity hunt myself and have developed a number of résumés.
3. I might look at the résumé development process from a different perspective than those résumé book guys.

Your résumé should be succinct, informative, accomplishment oriented, and neat.

It should be a snapshot of your business career.

The résumé should be unique. It should set itself apart from the rest. Although what's included in a résumé is the surest form of getting noticed, it's a good idea to differentiate it from others. Some people think a résumé on colored paper or unique paper stock is a way to go. Other's think that using a unique typeface or graphic design may be the direction.

These might all be true.

If you're an artist searching for some creative position, an artsy kind of résumé might be the ticket.

Then again, if you're in search of a more conservative business position, a conservative résumé might be the answer.

Notice how it is difficult for someone else to determine what is best for you?

Use your own instinct to develop what you believe is appropriate for you. The guiding principle is making it a great match for the opportunity.

Although a résumé might get you in the door for an interview, I have found that knowing someone already within a corporation (networking) is the best way to get an interview.

With networking, the résumé doesn't provide the impetus for the introduction, the acquaintance does. Thus a plain and simple résumé can suffice. Since you're already meeting the person, the résumé just supports your appearance and provides knowledge and background.

Whether or not you are using a résumé as an introduction tool may impact how the résumé is designed.

A business acquaintance once told me that a résumé sent out to corporate executives is received with the same enthusiasm and attention as junk mail.

Thus, if you do send a résumé, it must get noticed and "grab" the reader. I believe an objective of any résumé must be to remain in the mind of the reader after the reader has filed it away in his or her résumé drawer.

For that reason you're also well-advised to have the best cover letter possible to go with that BRP (best résumé possible).

And, sad to say, you are also well-advised to realize that the reward for all of your best efforts might be the garbage can.

With the advent of e-mail, the task simultaneously becomes easier and more difficult. Form is not as important as content. The importance of content is multiplied via e-mail.

In today's electronic environment, many who search through e-mail résumés are looking for keywords or phrases.

These words or phrases might get the applicant through the "first pass." Thus knowing the specifics of any open job opportunity can determine which phrases and words to use in order to get a résumé pulled out and noticed.

This is good news and bad news because in today's electronic message system, e-mail résumés can be sent out in the thousands within a short period of time. Employers are becoming slightly reticent in using this type of system to find viable candidates.

Since there are many job search engines, like Careers.com, Monster.com, etc., posting of résumés is like mass marketing.

And although that might be good for some job opportunities, it might be detrimental for others.

Your utilization of these sites might depend on the level of the job, the industry you're searching and how long you've been unemployed. Although mass e-mailing a résumé might be the way to go (based upon the number of career sites available), I believe face-to-face communication is critical. Call me old fashioned.

You Must Get in the Door

I have an old saying – well, it's not that old, but it is a saying – "You will never get a job or a new client if the individual doing the selection doesn't meet you in person."

Although the electronic age is running rampant in today's business environment, person-to-person communication is still the key component.

Personal interviews still determine who gets hired.

Thus, in my humble opinion, **the number-one objective of any résumé is to get an invitation to come into the company for a personal interview,** hopefully with the person who is responsible for the hiring.

You must get in the door to get any job or client.

And that usually means more than just a résumé.

That's why whether you send out mass résumés or are very selective and then follow up with a phone call, your only objective should be to get invited in for a personal meeting.

A personal meeting should be your only focus.

When I'm searching for new clients and I don't get a referral (it's just like a job interview), I don't send a brochure (a résumé).

I usually send a short note asking for a meeting.

If I get no response, I will follow up with a phone call and *only* ask to come in to meet the person.

I do this even if the meeting might only be for five minutes. Length of time doesn't matter. The key is getting in, in person.

Many candidates might be seeking the same position, so use your résumé to separate you from the pack. It might not be the document that gets you in, but that again is based upon individual cases.

So What Should Be in the Résumé?

We've talked about what your résumé should look like. Now let's talk about what you should include in it.

First of all, a résumé shouldn't be modest.

This, sometimes, is a tough hurdle to leap.

Most people are taught in business to be team oriented and that "there is no 'I' in team." That might be well and good when you're a part of a team, but when you're unemployed, remember there is an "I" in "hired." (Michael Jordan also noted that there is an "I" in "win.")

In the world of résumés, there is only "I." It's everyone for themselves. You're in competition with virtually every other candidate. You better act like it. So should your résumé.

That's why that résumé better focus on your accomplishments.

Don't be embarrassed to brag about your results. Being humble and showing a great deal of humility is usually not an asset when you're preparing a résumé and searching for an opportunity in a competitive marketplace.

Let's say you were in business for yourself and had a retail store. Then let's say a competitor opened up across the street. Would you let them alone, or would you fight back? If you don't fight back, you may soon be out of business.

The same thing holds true in résumé development. There are a number of competitors (other opportunity seekers) fighting for your position. Your résumé and your actions must be able to beat the competition.

So a little bit of bragging about what you've done can be a good thing and should be included. But be careful. Overbragging can be a negative. There's a fine line here, be cautious.

The résumé is a self-written business version of *This Is Your Life*. Like *This Is Your Life*, depending on your age and number of years in the working community, your résumé might be short or long. If you're looking for a first job with limited or no experience, then things you have done in your personal life might be important.

When I was growing up in Chicago I applied for a vendor's job (I was sixteen years old) at Wrigley Field (home of the great Chicago Cubs). I didn't have a written résumé at the time (I didn't even know what that was) and I had no experience, so I told them about my personal life. My mom and dad both worked. During summer break from school Wrigley Field became my babysitter – my mom and dad would send my brother and I to Cubs games so we wouldn't be home or on the streets alone "getting into trouble."

All games were day games, and since we lived a short train ride away, Wrigley Field was easy to get to.

I used that story to let them know that I knew every area within the ballpark and my knowledge would be a great asset when I was selling their products.

I would also be a great employee because I grew up as a Cubs fan – not always an easy thing in those days. I got the job.

Now, you're probably asking, "What does that story have to do with résumé development or getting a job?" It shows that when you're young (and sometimes even older), personal skills, initiative, and true-life stories that demonstrate you can meet the needs of the people you're talking to can influence the decision-making process.

As you get older and get more experience, your résumé will probably get longer and more informative. That's OK.

Use what's best for you. But don't forget the power of stories and the need to communicate that you want *this* job, not just *any* job.

Let's get back to what should be included.

Obviously include your name, address, home phone number, cell phone number, e-mail address, and any pertinent information about how you can be reached.

This might seem very basic, but I have seen a number of résumés without all of that information. And make sure you spell everything correctly. Have a friend proofread for typos, grammer, and spelling errors.

Remember, the spell checker isn't ideal for names, and it won't know the difference between "manager" and "manger."

Mistakes can easily be overlooked.

Make sure you catch any errors. About the only thing worse than a misspelled word is a prison record. Check. Double check. What the heck, triple check.

Next, include a summary of your background.

Here's an example from my own résumé. (Even though I have my own company, I've still created a résumé – or maybe I'll call it a "profile." Whatever you call it, you should always have one handy.)

Summary: A senior marketing and strategic planning executive with extensive experience in both multibillion dollar and entrepreneurial firms.

This includes a full range of planning and consultative activities: design, development, sales, and the implementation of myriad projects leading to more prosperous, dynamic, and profitable performance.

A highly creative, seasoned professional with a broad business background in a wide variety of industries, with a specialization in retailing and food service.

Wow, that sounded so good, I'd hire me (in fact, I did).

Next, and probably the longest part of your résumé, will be the experience part. This is where you list your jobs.

Start with the most recent position, and list the accomplishments you achieved at each company and position. This is where some bragging is quite acceptable. In fact, it's almost required.

You have to convince the reader that you did it and that you were not some innocent bystander hanging around while other people did the work.

Now, if you just graduated from college or high school and you have limited or no experience, you might list your education next instead of experience. But even summer jobs can be served up with some imagination.

Again, that is up to you. Your individual preferences should drive the bus, not what other people say or think.

Getting back to the experience section, try and be as succinct and accomplishment oriented as possible (but don't exaggerate.) In today's business environment, with so much unscrupulous behavior (see Tyco, Enron, Worldcom, etc.), it is important to stay above the misgivings of others.

If you've done it, list it; if you didn't do it, don't list it.

If you were a part of a team that accomplished something, say you were a part of that team and list what you did.

List all companies and positions you held within those companies. If you have a lot of experience and were with a number of companies and held numerous positions, just be detailed about the most current.

Since I did have a number of jobs and worked for a lot of companies, I just listed the company, title, and years of employment for positions I held a long time ago.

I graduated college in 1968, thus I listed only positions from 1968 to 1984. I got more specific after 1984.

That was just my preference. You might want to do something different, and that's OK. OK?

When you list your experience and accomplishments, again don't be afraid to brag and use descriptive words and phrases. Examples are: *Increased sales by 22%..., supervised a staff of…, developed budgets for…, aided in creating…, and spearheaded the team that…*

Try to use "action oriented" words like: *increased, supervised, developed, created, assisted, aided, spearheaded* (my favorite), *directed, guided,* etc.

All these can be used in a résumé to show off your talents.

Since you want to be noticed and selected over the competition (other candidates), providing an accurate picture of your experience and accomplishments is vital to your goal.

You don't have to be overly descriptive, either.

The résumé can be used to get you in the door. Once you're in you can take the time to expand on each one of your accomplishments in as much detail as the interviewer would like.

If you list everything in your résumé, what will be left for discussion when you meet the interviewer in person?

Next comes the important education section. If it was a long time ago, it doesn't have to be very elaborate, but it can be, depending on your educational accomplishments and if you graduated more recently.

As you grow older and have more jobs, the education section might be just a couple of lines. If you just graduated and were pretty accomplished in school, then list what you did.

From my own résumé, my education section was two lines: University of Illinois, Bachelors of Science Degree in Marketing and a Masters of Science in Advertising.

(In actuality, the only reason I listed it here is that maybe the University of Illinois will give me an honorarium for mentioning them. I could always use the money.)

Finally, your résumé should contain other bits and pieces of information you think would be of interest to the prospective interviewer or could assist you in getting a meeting or a leg up on the other candidates for the position you're applying for.

One strategy is to motivate the interviewer to meet with you because of similar interests or experiences. Membership in a fraternity or sorority can be very effective. Work with non-profit organizations can also help you find common ground with an interviewer.

If you're a volunteer at various venues, this might be included. In other words, list those things that you've done that might lead a reader to say, "This person looks like a valuable asset. We need to bring him in for an interview."

Many years ago, when job switching and downsizing weren't as prevalent, having a large number of different jobs during a career was considered to be a bad thing.

Employers would review a résumé, and if there were a lot of companies listed or an individual only worked a couple of months or a year or two at one company the applicant would be considered tainted.

Back then, if a person only worked for a company several months you could almost be assured that the job or company would not be listed on a résumé. It showed instability and a lack of commitment, thus the person creating the résumé would take a chance that this minor gap would not be noticed.

In today's business environment companies still like to see tenure and stability, but it's usually not the overriding factor as to whether an individual will receive a job offer.

Today companies want to see qualified talent. Hiring a person who, back in the day, was considered a "job hopper," is more acceptable than in the past.

So don't be afraid to list all the jobs, regardless of the number. Interviewers are more interested in what you've accomplished than the number of companies you've worked for. At least I believe that to be the rule today, rather than the exception.

Now don't get me wrong, there might be companies out there that still place a high emphasis on job stability. But like developing a résumé, it's an individual preference, and you have to adjust and adapt accordingly.

Variety Is Important

One other tip about creating your résumé. I'd recommend you work on developing more than one type of résumé.

Develop a specific résumé based on the needs of the company that is searching for a candidate and the qualifications and requirements of that position.

Let's say you decide you want to change industries and that for years you were in healthcare marketing. Now you want to explore another industry. Create a résumé that highlights what you did in the healthcare industry and show how that can be transferred to another industry.

A cover letter that reinforces the point will also be a good idea – and it should be part of the content in your follow-up phone call.

In many instances, the discipline (let's say marketing) you performed in one industry can be a valuable asset in another.

Don't be afraid to have a résumé stress that fact.

In many cases, having marketing experience in manufacturing might be an important selling point if you're now trying to get a marketing job in the retail industry.

Your résumé should reflect how your skills can transfer from one industry to another.

There is no law, rule, or guideline that says you must use the same résumé regardless of the job, position, or company you're applying for.

If you want to find a new opportunity in today's market place, be flexible. Have résumés available to reflect that flexibility. Position-specific résumés will place you above the other candidates and provide you with a better chance of finding that new opportunity.

So there you have it, how to develop and use your résumé to your advantage when searching for that new exciting opportunity. I want to reiterate the points of this stage:

- First, you must have a résumé if you plan to find a new opportunity.
- Second, how the résumé is developed, the style you use, what's included, etc., should be up to you. Don't be concerned about using reference materials to assist you in its development.
- Finally, create a variety of different résumés to meet the specific needs of the opportunities you're searching for, the industries and the companies you're targeting. Use your résumé as an asset, not a liability.

Although the résumé is an important tool to get a new opportunity, you won't get anything unless you get in to meet the person doing the hiring.

And that means cover letters and follow-up phone calls.

While you're working on your résumé, there is something else you have to do.

It's time to take the next step. Take a deep breath, clear your head, and head up or down to the unemployment office.

This is the next necessary step as you traverse the seven stages of successful unemployment.

Good luck.

You're about to begin dealing with a government agency…

You'll need all the luck you can get.

Stage Four... Getting Your Unemployment Benefits

"There ain't no such thing as a free lunch."

If you've ever dealt with a government office or agency before, you know the fun is about to begin. If you haven't, start your engines because you're about to set off for a very important and maybe stressful journey.

This is the moment you must traverse the red tape obstacle course set up by the government as you try and negotiate and complete all the steps necessary to begin receiving your unemployment benefits.

(An interesting combination of terms...how can unemployment be a benefit? Just asking.)

If you've never done this, and I hope you never have, you're in for the memory of a lifetime. Remember, this is a government agency. Is it necessary to say anything more? Of course – otherwise this would be a very short chapter.

No Matter What State You're In...

I must mention a point or two about this stage. Since there are fifty states (at last count) there's a real good chance that each state has its own slightly different method or process set up for you to register and collect your unemployment benefits.

Some might be totally automated, some might require you to visit the unemployment office in person, and still others might have a combination of the two. Since I was only unemployed in one state (at last count), I can only relate to you the one process I'm familiar with.

It is my advice that as soon as you become unemployed, find out the requirements in your state. Then, follow the process diligently.

A brief historical note. It used to be called the unemployment office. I guess the government thought that was too negative. So they've changed the name to the State Workforce Commission – at least in the state I'm in. I think I'll start collecting a state-by-state listing of what they call it and what their procedures are – look for it in the next edition!

The Government's Version of Catch-22

The unemployment office is made up of people who are employed. Their main job is to service the needs of the unemployed. In other words, these people are employed because you're unemployed.

And although I'm certain some of them are truly compassionate and want to assist, they have rules and regulations they must abide by if they want to stay employed. So no matter how stupid these rules seem, the employed personnel in the unemployment office are there to make certain all the rules and regulations are followed to the letter of the law. Their jobs depend on it.

In all honesty, to them, you're a paycheck. If it weren't for you, they would be unemployed.

It's sort of the government's version of the book *Catch-22*. If you're unemployed, then they're employed. But if you're not unemployed, then they might be. Thus, they would rather have you be unemployed than themselves. Got it?

If they became unemployed, then the government would probably have to hire other people to process their claims. Thus, no matter who is unemployed, someone who is employed will be working for the government unemployment office checking and processing claims.

All part of the Master Plan, I guess.

What's First?

This depends on the state in which you reside. In the past, everyone had to personally visit the office and register to qualify for benefits.

In your state that might continue to be the case. In my state (I'm not telling) a personal visit is no longer required. The entire process is handled via automated telephone or online.

However, if you reside in a state where you must visit in person, the day you decide to visit the unemployment office, if it's your first time, will be an interesting experience.

Not knowing any better, you will probably dress as if you were going to the office, just to be impressive (I did). Suit and tie or a nice skirt and blouse. The things you wore when you were employed, if that is what you wore. You might just wear "business casual," the dress code of many offices today.

A tip …this is not necessary.

Remember, since you're visiting a government agency, you might have to wait for long periods of time in line with people who have already made their initial visit to the unemployment office. They will be dressed as if they are on vacation, which in reality they are, sort of.

Thus, dressing up is not necessary.

The clerks or counselors who you will meet to "get processed" won't care one way or the other what you wear. So dress comfortably. They get paid regardless of what you wear.

Your first exposure should be brief. You will enter a reception line and eventually a receptionist will greet you. "Name and social security number!"

So you provide the receptionist with the necessary information about yourself.

They enter your info into a computer, and in seconds your entire work history is flashed on a screen. Who you worked for, when you worked for them, and how much money you earned while you were employed by them. (Nothing in this world is confidential.)

After this brief encounter, you get a piece of paper that tells you when to come back for counseling and processing. This is normally within the same week.

That's it, your first visit is over.

Really exciting, huh?

A Step Back

Before I move on, we need to take a step backward. As I mentioned earlier, each state has its own process for handling claims. What I reviewed in the "What's First?" section is how it used to be done.

It still might be done that way in your state. However, with the advent of automated phone systems and the Internet, many states have moved in an automated direction to eliminate the in-office hassles and long waiting lines filled with potentially irate or depressed applicants.

The important thing to remember is that receiving unemployment insurance benefits is your right as a worker. But it's also your responsibility to make sure you do all that's required to receive these benefits.

Unemployment Insurance (Benefits)

Unemployment insurance is an employer-paid insurance program that assists workers who are unemployed through no fault of their own. This is a key definition. *No fault of their own.*

That means if you get fired for unscrupulous behavior or poor performance or some such, or you decide to quit, for whatever reason, you're *not* eligible for benefits. Again, it must be for no fault of your own.

A Few More Facts

Employer taxes and reimbursements support the unemployment trust fund. Employers cannot deduct any money from their employee wages to pay for this program.

Since these benefits are paid to you by your past employer, through the government, remember that all of your benefits are taxable at the end of the calendar year. (Isn't that just like the government? You get benefits because you're not working and you really need the money, and they tax you for receiving it. Go figure.)

The Process

If you get downsized, you must notify the unemployment office of your situation. Your notification begins to set up the process for you to receive benefits.

Since you're dealing with the government, there are certain rules and regulations you must adhere to in order to receive your benefits.

Regardless of your financial situation, you should apply.

Again, it is your right. It might be difficult to admit you're unemployed, but get over it as soon as possible (see the one-week mourning period in the "Welcome" chapter) and register.

The process is a lot simpler than it was in the past, but it still can take time. As I mentioned earlier, it might be in-person, via phone, online, or a combination of the three.

Filing a Claim

In my state all claims are handled online or over the phone. I recommend you make a phone call to begin the process. If you want to talk to someone in person about filing, forget about it.

In the FAQ brochure you get from the unemployment office it states:

Q: "Can I speak to someone in person about my claim?"
A: "All unemployment insurance services are handled online or by telephone only."

So you better be proficient in punching numbers on a phone or be proficient with the Internet, your only options.

I suggest you use a regular landline telephone, not a cell phone. You will be punching in a bunch of numbers. Having the numbers next to your ear can make the process cumbersome. (That's one of those wonderful tips you won't get anywhere else but in this book.)

Once you register, which lets the government know of your situation, they will send a claim questionnaire to your past employer.

Your employer must fill it out and send it back.

From that point on, you're in the system. The employer must verify that you were laid off, not fired or quit on your own accord, although there are circumstances whereby if you quit you might still receive benefits.

In addition, your previous employer will provide the government office a wage history so the government can determine the benefits you will receive.

After the office receives the questionnaire back from your past employer, you will receive a statement of benefits, which will tell you the following information:
- the four completed calendar quarters used for your claim (the base period);
- the wages your employer(s) reported paying you during each quarter;
- whether you're eligible for benefit amounts based on those wages; and
- your benefit amounts if you qualify to receive them.

The weekly benefit amount is what you will receive for one full week of unemployment. It is based on the total earnings of the highest of the four completed quarters.

The maximum benefit amount is the total amount you can receive during your active claim year.

Although I'm not sure if each state's benefit amount is different (I don't think it is), as of this printing, it is my understanding that the weekly benefit you can receive based upon past wages ranges from a minimum of $53 per week to a maximum of $330 per week.

(These figures do change periodically.)

These amounts will not place you in "tall cotton," but believe me, if it is all that you're getting, it seems like the mother lode.

Qualifications

State qualifications may vary, but for you to receive benefits you must meet certain requirements in three main areas. By the way, you must meet *all* of these requirements:

- You must have enough wages in the first four of the last five completed calendar quarters before you filed your claim. (This is based on some formula that is confusing to me.)
- You must be unemployed or partially unemployed through no fault of your own.
  There are some exceptions in this area:
    - You were fired without work-related misconduct.
    - You quit your job for a good work-related or medical reason.
    - You quit your job to move with your spouse.
  If these reasons exist, you might still be eligible for benefits. (See your state's regulations for more details.)
- You must be physically able and available to work full-time. You must be actively seeking full-time work and keep a detailed record of your work search activities.

There is some good news here. If you're temporarily laid off and you have a definite return-to-work date, you might not be required to search for work.

Make certain you find out all the necessary details.

Also, in order to continue to receive benefits you must:
- try and get a face-to-face interview every day; and
- try to get two or more job searching contacts per week.

You can phone, e-mail, send résumés, attend job fairs, or whatever.

Another important point. If you are to keep receiving your benefits you *must* register for work at your local unemployment office or complete an online job application. This work registration must be completed within seven (7) days from filing your claim. Registering for work and filing a claim are two separate and distinct steps.

Getting Paid

So you've filled out your claim, you've registered for work, you've reviewed your statement of benefits, and you've been approved to receive your benefits. When will you receive your first check? (By the way, it can't come soon enough.)

In most instances, you will receive your first check during the third or fourth week following your initial claim filing. Thus, the faster you begin the unemployment registration process, the better.

Now, you're probably wondering how much will your benefits be, how big will that first check be, and how long does this windfall last?

Let's take one question at a time…

First Question: How much will my benefits be?

Your statement of benefits should tell you how much you will receive on a weekly basis. Review it carefully.

It is based on information the government has received from your past employer(s). If there is a mistake, you can call the office and find out how to get this figure adjusted.

Second Question: How much will my first check be?

The amount of this check will depend on your earnings.

The law requires that the government hold the payment of the first payable week as the waiting period week. So, essentially, your first check will be for the second payable week.

All future checks will be for two payable weeks.

The simplest explanation is that you will receive your withheld week of pay after you have exhausted your remaining unemployment insurance benefits.

Third Question: How long does this windfall last?

The maximum time allowable to collect your benefits is twenty-six weeks, but the law states you have one full calendar year to receive those benefits. Thus if you get wages from a job while receiving benefits, these wages will be deducted from your benefits, using some type of formula.

This reduction of payments allows you to extend your benefits time period. The key is the money, not the time period, as long as it is within a one-year calendar period.

It is also important to tell you how you will receive your checks. Again, this might vary from state to state, but here it is done by the following method.

You request payment by filing a claim certification. You get instructions that tell you whether to file by calling the automated phone system or by filing a paper claim certification.

Filing claims by phone is a piece of cake. Simply call the automated system anytime on your designated day once every two weeks. Punch in your social security number and answer yes or no to a bunch of questions. It takes about four minutes and in two to four weeks your benefit check is in the mail.

One last point: the job search log. In order to keep receiving your benefits you must participate in an active job search.

In my state that means you must keep an active job search log. This is provided to you by the unemployment office.

In this log you must provide the following: the date, employer name, address and phone number, how the employer was contacted, who you contacted, what kind of work was sought and the salary requirements, the results, and did you fill out an application and file a résumé. This log must be current and updated regularly.

The government can audit this log on a random basis at any time, thus it is to your advantage to keep it current. If you don't live up to this requirement, you can lose your benefits. That said, a friend of mine has filed for unemployment three times, in two states, over the last twenty years. He was *never* asked to provide a job search log. In fact, the worker at his last unemployment office actually told him, "Don't worry about keeping a log, we never check them."

Be aware, your unemployment office might ask for your log, so keep it current.

Is That All?

What you've just read covers most of the process.

Again, it might be different in your state. So please make sure that once you're notified of your situation, you contact your local unemployment office and follow their procedures.

If you're not happy with your statement of benefits or anything else that occurs while you're receiving benefits, there is a three-level appeal process.

If you lose level one, go to level two, and so on. Make sure you utilize the entire system available to you.

If you're turned down for benefits, make sure you appeal. You have nothing to lose. Who knows, things might change.

The government is not here to cheat you. They really do want to assist you as much as possible within what the law allows.

In my state there is an in-depth unemployment insurance information brochure available to all personnel. I'm sure there's one for your state, too. Make certain you get a copy of it. It contains a tremendous amount of useful information that will help you get through this process with a lot less stress. And you've already got too much stress.

Sections of my brochure include: How Do I Qualify? How Do I Claim Weeks of Unemployment? What Are My Ongoing Requirements? Is My Claim Confidential? What If Wages Are Missing or Wrong? How Do I File an Appeal? How Does the Appeal Process Work? Special Circumstances That Apply to Some People, and a whole lot more.

Now, besides providing benefits, the unemployment office also provides job search seminars, a list of available openings, computer facilities, and much more. They are doing what they can to get you employed and off the unemployment rolls.

Utilize as much of their services as you think you need, but remember, if you're searching for a "high level" position, I'm not sure all of the tips and leads will be helpful.

The key to finding a new, exciting business opportunity is to go out and make it happen.

Going out and finding a job is a full-time job.

Utilize all the information available to you to ensure you do all you can to find that new opportunity.

Developing a strategic plan that can help you determine where you want to go and how you will get there is the next stage.

The sooner this is realized, the faster and better your chances are of finding that new business opportunity or job.

So now we come to the next stage in the process…

Creating a Plan…

Stage Five...
Creating a Plan

"Trying to run a business without a strategic plan is like shooting into the forest and hoping dinner runs into the bullets."

Plan…you hear the word all of the time.

"We must have a comprehensive plan."

"Our plan during the war was to…"

"Those who fail to plan, plan to fail…"

So if it is so important, what is a plan?

Webster's dictionary defines "plan" as "a method for achieving an end." Duh. A bit simplistic, but correct.

Basically, a plan is a way to accomplish something. In this case, finding a new opportunity or job. A way to move forward.

Many years ago I came across a literary work about a plan.

As far as I know, the author is unknown. It's such a good work I thought I'd include it here before we move on to the discussion of developing a plan.

It certainly clarifies what a plan is.

It's called, oddly enough… "The Plan."

It goes like this…

The Plan

In the beginning was the plan.

And then came the assumptions.

And the assumptions were without form.

And the plan was completely without substance.

And darkness was upon the face of the workers.

And they spake unto their marketing manager, saying, *"It is a pot of crap, and it stinketh."*

And the marketing manager went unto the strategists and sayeth, *"It is a pile of dung, and none may abide by the odor thereof."*

And the strategists went unto the business managers and sayeth unto them, *"It is a container of excrement, and it is very strong, such that none may abide by it."*

And the business managers went unto the director and sayeth unto him, *"It is a vessel of fertilizer, and none may abide its strength."*

And the director went unto the vice president and sayeth, *"It contains that which aids plant growth, and it is very strong."*

And the vice president went unto the senior vice president and sayeth, *"It promoteth growth, and it is powerful."*

And the senior vice president went unto the president and sayeth unto him, *"This powerful new plan will actively promote growth and efficiency of the company and the business in general."*

And the president looked upon the plan and saw it was good.

And the Plan Became Policy.

Why present that literary work? It shows that a plan, even if it's bad, can turn into something good with the proper spin.

You need to guard against developing a bad plan that will hinder you in getting your new opportunity by seeming to be a good one.

Your Plan Is Vital for Survival

The development of a plan is really an organization of thoughts. It is a methodical approach to thinking. It is a way to get you from point A to point B.

The plan of attack is absolutely the most vital step you will take in finding a new business opportunity.

Without a viable plan you are in danger of creating an environment where you wander aimlessly, reacting to situations rather than proactively taking steps that will lead you to viable job opportunities.

Plan Creation

Like résumé development, there are hundreds of opinions on how to develop a plan. You should use the approach that best suits your needs. However, to get you going, I thought I would provide you with some methods that worked well for me when I was in the market.

Write It Down

First and foremost you must understand that developing a plan does not have to be a difficult process. But regardless of whether it is a simple or complex plan, it *must be written down*.

The development of a plan might be a time-consuming process, but even though it might be, it will be some of the most productive time you will spend. Your plan should be created before you begin your active opportunity search.

Take the time to do it right before you begin your hunting, and you will see how much time and energy and possibly money you will save as you begin your job hunting or business opportunity journey.

Almost every successful company has some sort of written plan they refer to, to determine where they are going and if they are on the right track.

Be Realistic

As you begin to develop your plan, make sure it is as realistic as possible. It will provide you comfort and sanity.

You must realize that the process of finding a new opportunity can take quite some time.

There are articles daily in the newspaper about individuals who have been searching for a new opportunity for more than a year with no positive results. Sometimes these individuals "fall out" of the job market because they are frustrated that nothing has turned up.

I can't tell you whether they have written plans or not, but I know from my own experience that having a written plan can compress the time needed to find a job or new business opportunity. If your plan doesn't compress the time, you can at least prepare for the delay by developing a course of action. In other words, plan for it.

What Should the Plan Include?

Many plans have both short-term and long-term goals. I suggest that in your particular circumstance you stick to the short-term goals – what you should do now and within the next six months.

When creating a plan, be prepared to include the following information: who, what, where, when, why, and how.

Utilizing these catagories will organize your thoughts and provide you with the necessary tools to clarify your plan. I reiterate: a plan doesn't have to be complex, although it should be as thorough as possible.

The reason I use this process is that it worked for me.

Who...

Who do you plan to make contact and meet with as you begin your search? Remember, the key to finding a new opportunity is to make contact with as many people as you can. List names, companies, phone numbers, positions, e-mail addresses, how you know them, etc. These contacts will be crucial as you begin your search. No one you know should be left off this list.

What...

What kind of positions and opportunities will you be seeking? What industries will you be exploring? What are your qualifications that will place you in a positive position to get the job?

Also, what kind of competition is out there vying for the same opportunities? In other words, what other candidates will you be competing against for possible positions and what is the best way to prove to a prospective employer that you're better qualified.

Where...

Where do you plan to look for these new opportunities?

Where are the identified Internet search engines, newspaper ads, bulletin boards, employment agencies, recruitment firms, etc. If the industry that you've been employed in is undergoing a major downsizing, are there other industries that can utilize your talents? Where are these companies?

Do you plan to relocate? If so, where?

Remember, if you cannot relocate, the time it takes to find a new opportunity might expand.

Plan for that occurrence.

When...

When should you begin your search?

This might seem foolish, but if you're currently employed and are unhappy or just realize it's time to change, this is when you should begin to plan for your search.

If you know a reduction is inevitable and you might be a part of it, do you wait for some type of severance package?

If there is no severance package, do you wait on the hope that you won't be downsized?

Why...

If you're already unemployed, the *why* is simple.

But what if you're currently employed and you're unhappy or you notice the warning signals referred to earlier?

Is this motivation enough for you to begin a job search?

That is why a plan is so useful. It can provide you with the necessary input and motivation to get moving.

The plan itself won't move you, but creating the plan will provide you with the time and structure to reflect on your current position. Creating the plan will also help you develop various options that will be included in your plan.

How...

How will you proceed in finding your new opportunity?

You will list, and then utilize very specific steps to get yourself out of the clutches of unemployment and into the grasp of a new job.

Obviously, there are many methods you can use to find a new opportunity, and you probably should use all of them.

But remember, certain methods are better than others.

The ones that usually take little time are the ones that are least successful. Methods that take time and might be cumbersome are usually productive.

Your plan should prioritize methods by their productivity. Target the most productive methods first.

For example, networking (which will be discussed in the next stage) is by far the best approach.

Contacting everyone you know and asking them if they know of an opportunity can lead to a new career.

Your plan should account for this.

You should also explore mass e-mailing, recruitment firms, newspapers ads, employment offices, trade journals, etc.

Realize, though, that the least amount of effort to perform any task will probably provide the least opportunity for finding a new opportunity.

However, your plan should include every option for exploration. You never know – the one that the experts say is the worst might turn out to be your best.

Since finding a new opportunity is a numbers game, leave no stone unturned. Just plan for it accordingly.

The Plan Format

As mentioned earlier, there are a variety of ways to plan and there are hundreds of formats you can use.

The Internet can provide you with a variety of formats.

You can search Lycos, Ask Jeeves, Google, etc., and probably get what you need.

In this instance, I don't believe your plan has to be extremely structured. The main purpose of the plan is to provide methodical thinking and offer a means of identifying the process to find a job opportunity.

I have found the who, what, where, when, why, and how format to be very beneficial.

It forces you to ask yourself the basic questions.

At least to begin with, I suggest you use it, too.

The Budget

There is one other section that needs to be included in your plan. That is a budget section.

This is important because being unemployed can have a huge financial impact on you and on your family's life.

You must confront the budget issues and deal with them accordingly. Understanding what you must spend and what you bring in will help you cope with your situation and take some of the stress off your job search.

Again, the budget section doesn't have to be complicated, just thorough. You must try and list every expense item so that you know exactly how much money will be going out the door each month.

Be as itemized as you possibly can.

Some of the items that probably should be included are items related to:

- Housing
- Food
- Clothing
- Transportation
- Medical and prescription drug expenses
- Education
- Insurance costs
- Credit cards and other debts
- Federal, state, and local taxes
- Discretionary spending (if applicable)

List every item you can think of that will have a drain on you financial resources.

Next list all the income that will be coming in monthly.

For example, if you have a severance package, unemployment benefits, your spouse's and children's income (if they are employed), stock dividends or interest earned on investments, part-time job income, money from relatives (loans), etc. Again, be as thorough as possible.

Compare your income earned with your expenses to determine your net profit or loss. If it is a loss, you might have to develop areas in your plan where you will cut back in order to survive during this unemployed period in your life.

Including a budget as a part of your plan will provide you the opportunity to at least cope with your financial dilemma and operate within your financial limitations.

Be Focused

While you're in the process of planning, it is important to take some time and perform some type of due diligence.

This due diligence is a means of performing an introspective evaluation of your own career and capabilities (both strengths and weaknesses) to determine if you have the proper tools for the specific jobs that might become available.

It is a way of matching your skills to the opportunities.

This review is recommended because you might be under a lot of pressure to get a job.

Instead of creating a viable plan, you might go out and apply for any position that you might appear to be qualified for even though you know you're not.

Pressure makes people do many irrational things, and this might certainly be one of them.

For example, if all of your training and past positions have been in the high-tech industry as an engineer, it would be a waste of time to send a résumé for the position of sales manager in the fashion industry.

Now you might think your skills are transferable, but the person reviewing your résumé would look at it and probably laugh.

It is a waste of everybody's time to apply for a position that you know you're not qualified for, but the pressure of finding a new opportunity can be intense and so you do things you wouldn't normally do.

If you see a job listing and by reading the qualifications and requirements you know you're not qualified for it, don't send a résumé for the position.

First of all, if you send your résumé via e-mail, it won't even be noticed, and second, if it is mailed, the initial reviewer (who in many cases might be an assistant or such) will look for specific qualifications, and it won't get past them.

What you've done by sending in the résumé is gotten your hopes up that you will be contacted, and when you're not, rejection rears its ugly head.

If you've created a viable plan that is specific about your qualifications and requirements, you won't react to these situations. Your time and effort will be more efficient, targeted so that a payoff (a new offer or new business opportunity) can come quicker. That is the purpose of the plan.

The most important advice I can provide in this stage is to take the time to create the plan before you spend a great deal of time searching for that new opportunity. In other words, organize your thoughts and actions so they are not wasted.

I mentioned earlier in this book that when unemployment occurs you should give yourself a week to mourn and then move on. That week might be the perfect time to create your plan.

While you're in this mourning period, sit back, take a deep breath, relax, and begin creating a plan of attack to find that new business opportunity.

This can be a useful, productive tool to assist you in getting over the mourning period. Once it is over, you can be revitalized and rejuvenated, resulting in you getting the position or opportunity you desire.

Even though I have listed creating a plan as Stage Five in the seven stages, you might find it rewarding or necessary to place this stage near the front of the process. That's fine.

My main purpose here is to motivate you to create that plan, regardless of where it's positioned in this book.

So let's review…

You've learned how to put up a positive front and realize that you're not alone when it comes to being unemployed.

We've provided you with input to accept the fact that you're unemployed and that you must move forward, positively.

You've developed (you hope) a dynamite résumé or résumés that you'll use to provide interviewers with the information they need to make a positive hiring decision about you.

We've touched on what needs to be done to begin collecting that unemployment compensation you so rightly deserve.

We've just given you the necessary input and tools and motivation to begin creating a plan for becoming employed again.

Now we begin the next stage of the journey and that is... *making it happen.*

Stage Six... Making It Happen

"You can stand on the dock and watch, or you can get in the boat and row."

It's Not Always Your Fault

Throughout this book I've tried to prepare you for what it feels like to be unemployed and what you need to do to move from unemployment to that new job or business opportunity.

We now come to the part where the rubber meets the road. Making it happen.

I can understand your thought process. It happened to me.

You think to yourself, "If I did my job better," "If I just stayed late for that meeting," "If I'd landed that one big account."

If… If… If… Well, maybe yes, but probably not.

It probably has more to do with today's economy and the company you used to work for than it has to do with you.

Just because you're unemployed or might be headed in that direction (in many cases without even knowing it) doesn't mean it was your fault.

I can list a dozen or more people (it might even be hundreds of people) who have lost their jobs because they got caught up in the numbers reduction continuum. I bet you can, too.

How many times have you seen headlines that read "So and so company to reduce staff by 7%" or "XYZ Corporation to downsize by 7,500 people."

It's almost a daily occurrence. Do you really believe that all those employees did something wrong to justify their dismissal? Of course not.

When management realizes that expense reductions are required, that's usually what happens. "The company is taking a one-time write-off to account for our actions." Voluntary cutbacks are offered, early retirement is suggested, and if all else fails, general layoffs occur. Management decides who gets laid off depending on the need of the position, the usefulness of the department, etc.

Often, it's not even an individual employee issue. I've seen all too many cases where entire plants close down and all the people employed are laid off, regardless of their individual performance.

Except in cases where poor performance or unscrupulous behavior occurs, most executives find the reduction of staff an agonizing move. But sometimes it just has to be done.

So you just can't sit around all day and mope. You must begin to act and act now! As I stated earlier, you're not alone. Millions of individuals are in the same boat. So the competition to find a new opportunity may be massive and intense.

Opportunities can come and go quickly. Besides having the right qualifications and, in many cases, knowing the right people, timing is often key in finding a new opportunity.

That's why waiting and feeling sorry for yourself can be detrimental to your objective of finding a new opportunity.

Networking Is the Answer

If you want to make things happen, *you and only you* will make it so. One of the surest ways to make things happen is through networking. I'm certain you've heard this before. But it deserves repeating.

Networking is the surest means of finding a new job or business opportunity. Like résumé development, there are a number of books on the market suggesting a variety of ways to network. No matter how you do it, it will be the most or one of the most beneficial steps you take in moving forward to that new opportunity.

But what exactly is networking? Networking, as defined by Webster, "is the exchange of information or services among individuals, groups, or institutions." In its simplest form, it is the means of telling a lot of people you're searching for a new business opportunity or job.

You hope they know of a job or know a person who knows a person, etc., who might be aware of an opportunity.

The Hidden Market

Experts call this the "hidden job market." However, this can also be applicable if you've decided to form your own company or are looking for a business to purchase. Letting a bunch of people know what you're trying to accomplish can compress the time line dramatically.

Think of your own situation. When you were employed, how many people who worked with you got their job because they knew someone within the company? I'll bet if you do extensive research, you will find out it's a lot.

That's the way it is in today's business environment. As stated in the prelude, one of my "life lessons learned" is it's not what you know, but who you know. Or as they say in Chicago, "Don't send nobody nobody sent." Who you know is the key to a new opportunity. That's what networking is all about.

Let me provide an actual example. I'm sure you can think of your own. Anyway, I know several people who were employed with a company in financial difficulty.

All were in upper management, and the board of directors made a decision that in order to survive, they had to find a buyer. After an extensive search, the board found a purchaser, and the company was sold.

Immediately, several individuals from the upper management team were asked to resign. A new chief executive officer was hired, and within a couple of weeks after her arrival, the remaining upper management team was requested to resign.

Why? The financial difficulty was not upper management's fault to begin with.

The reason they all "left" was because the new CEO was not familiar with the team, so she brought in her own team, people who worked with her somewhere in the past.

The past upper management team performed well, but she didn't know them and didn't want to take the time to know them. She was interested in bringing in her own team to "move the company forward as quickly as possible."

She can't be blamed for her actions.

The point of this story is that through her past acquaintances she was able to form a team she was more comfortable with and the previous team was let go. Through her network of executives, she formed a new team and moved forward.

If you were unemployed at that time (or even if you were employed) and you knew and worked with her in the past and you contacted her to let her know you were available and she had faith and trust in you, the chances would be above average that you would be hired.

Networking would get you in the door, and if the need was there...*poof*, you got the job. And that window of opportunity was a fairly brief one. This is not an uncommon example or an isolated illustration.

People want to be around people they know and can count on. With strangers, you roll the dice. In today's business environment, people no longer want to take the chance. They want a sure thing, so they have a tendency to hire people they know and trust.

Even if a company relies on a corporate recruiter, if you look far enough in the past, their paths probably crossed.

Networking is the key to opening up the door to a new and brighter future. It can be the way to find job happiness. It can be the motivation behind making it happen.

Why Networking?

How do we know networking is right for you? Let's say you've never done it before and, for example purposes, you're a bit of an introvert. How can it be used to your advantage? How can you become proficient in networking?

First of all, almost everyone has done some sort of networking in their life. When you were dating, you may have used networking to find a date.

If you had a friend whose date was a pretty cool person, or even if not, you might have asked your friend if his or her date could fix you up with a friend. Instead of going to the bars or church socials or other singles functions, you asked your friend to introduce you to some available people. That's networking.

You made an assumption that since your friend was dating a cool person, that person would know other cool people, and a hook-up occurred. That's networking.

So how do you go about networking and setting up a network of individuals to find you that new opportunity? That's what this stage is all about. Networking is a method of using personal contacts to meet people. Not only is it possible to get a date through networking, you probably used it for other things, too.

If you moved to a new city and you needed a doctor, how did that come about? Didn't you ask a business associate, a neighbor, or a friend to recommend one? When you needed an attorney or a CPA, didn't you ask around for a name or two? When you needed some work done around the house – painting, plumbing, roofing – didn't you ask people for a referral? Most likely, you did.

Well, if you asked for names of people in those examples, why wouldn't you use the same method for finding a new opportunity? That's what networking is all about. And that's what you're going to do.

So if you want to make contact with a person who might be hiring, you're going to have to do some networking – maybe a lot of networking.

In networking, no one is off limits. You should try and contact almost everyone you know. And then don't be afraid to ask them for some names to expand your network. That's how you get jobs.

Networking is a very personal experience. You're asking for help. Sometimes this is very difficult to do. When a negative situation occurs, like unemployment, it is usually not something that people like to talk about. But then again, what better time to ask for help than when you actually need it?

Here's an interesting phenomenon. People will go out of their way to help you when you need it, but you have to let them know that you need help.

The Networking Process

The first step in the networking process is to let people know about your situation.

You may feel embarrassed about it. But you have to get over it. People can only help you if they know you need help.

If you keep your situation to yourself or keep it hidden from people other than your family and close friends, your chances of network expansion and finding a new opportunity are very limited.

In today's environment, where unemployment is a more and more common occurrence, there are a number of networking functions that are held daily, weekly, or monthly.

Different organizations sponsor networking meetings. Many are held in churches, synagogues, social halls, etc. Make sure you look for these announcements, usually in the newspaper or on the Internet, and attend these functions.

These are multipurpose events. They provide input, support, and a forum to meet other people in your situation – so that you will feel less depressed and alone.

You'll get the opportunity to meet other people who might be in similar circumstances. These people, even though they might be unemployed, know people who you probably don't know. They can be an excellent source of names and strategies for networking.

Remember what I said earlier? Even though one department or group of departments in a company might be laying off, other departments in the same company may be hiring. So if the people you meet at a networking meeting are in the technology department and were downsized, that doesn't mean the entire company is undergoing massive layoffs. For example, they might need salespeople.

Another good thing about networking meetings is that they often bring in speakers who are experts in areas where you might need assistance. They might have a speaker on résumé development, interview techniques, or on budgeting.

They may have a psychologist who discusses the feelings that you might be experiencing now that unemployment has touched you. These meetings can be extremely worthwhile because they can act as a support system, and any type of support you can get is positive.

If you're a member of an association or society, let the other members know of your circumstance. These organizations usually hold monthly or quarterly meetings. Attend them regularly and ask for assistance. I belong to a number of different groups, and at every meeting there are at least two or three people who, when introduced, let us know they are "in transition."

Above all, remain positive, because that positive attitude will be a big asset when you begin to set up meetings and expand your own network. Once you begin the networking process, you will be amazed at the responses you will get and the assistance some individuals are willing to supply.

So make sure you let people know. Begin with relatives, neighbors, business associates, church members, etc. Discuss your situation with people at the company that just let you go.

They know people you don't know, and they might be willing to assist and provide a reference. Heck, they may be next in line and might need your help in the future.

Making these initial contacts can be stressful and might take a bit of courage, but don't let that stop you. You have to get out there. And you must do it now.

Start making every contact you can. No one is off limits. No matter how remote you think the contact is to the business world, you will be surprised what might turn up.

In fact, there is some research that indicates that weak relationships often pay off better than strong ones. What do they mean by that? It seems that the "friend of a friend" or even the "friend of a friend of my cousin's friend" type of connections and referrals can end up paying off better than the really close relationships.

It's one of the reasons that networking seems to work. So don't just look in the obvious places and don't stop with close friends. That's just the start.

I'll bet you have lots of places to look that you might not have thought of. For example, I assume you get your hair cut. Right? Let your barber or hair stylist know of your situation – especially if you've been going to the same person for several years. Since other people also get haircuts, it might turn out that one of your stylist's other clients is looking for people.

It's not as remote as it sounds.

After all, your barber wants to keep you as a paying customer – so he'll be motivated, too.

Other examples of remote networking opportunities are the local supermarket, the place where you get your car repaired, and sales personnel you might know at local boutiques or department stores that you or your spouse frequent.

Don't forget your lawyer and accountant – if you have one.

If you have a favorite restaurant where most of the employees know you, that can be another opportunity.

Your banker can be another source. In other words, as I have stated before, it's time to get the word out – nothing is too unconventional or remote.

OK, let's have a quick review. You've started the process of notifying everyone you know of your situation. You're attending networking meetings, you're searching the classifieds, you're logging on to all the job search engines via the Internet, and you're exploring all possible avenues where jobs might be listed.

Congratulations, you've become a proactive networker.

The next step in the networking process is making the contacts. That sounds simple enough. You'll write letters or e-mail all the people you know to tell them of your situation, and once they realize your dilemma you'll get more meetings and offers than you'll know what to do with. *Ha Ha Ha Ha!*

Pardon my laughter, but this is a very unrealistic expectation.

Positive Attitude vs. Unrealistic Expectations

Don't get me wrong, as mentioned earlier, having a positive attitude is essential in the new opportunity search process, but unrealistic expectations are not.

If you have unrealistic expectations, you only set yourself up for perceived failure and depression.

Unrealistic expectations can also imply to your family support group that you're not in a tough situation and you'll find a new opportunity within several weeks or months.

If you don't meet that goal, frustration will set in from all members of your support group. That could lead to conflict.

Finally, your own credibility with your close support group is the final casualty.

Expecting a large number of contacts and offers in a short period of time is unrealistic. That doesn't mean it shouldn't be a goal, but keep that goal to yourself.

My recommendation is to prepare a more realistic time line, with the understanding that finding a new opportunity can take quite a bit of time. Now, if you want to have a more aggressive time line in your subconscious, that's OK. But keep it to yourself.

Now here's a bit of good news. In the past, people who were employed really didn't believe they would be in your situation, so most of them wouldn't go far out of their way to help and, in many cases, viewed job loss as being somehow "your fault." In addition, it's just not a top priority for someone who is working to help someone who isn't.

Take your own behavior when you were employed. Unless you're an exception to the rule, you didn't spend an exorbitant amount of time visiting and helping people who were networking to find a job or new opportunity. You were too busy.

A report was due yesterday. You were going out of town on business and wouldn't be back for a week. When you got back you were bombarded with work because of recent cutbacks.

You didn't want to be a part of the second wave, so you didn't have much time to meet people who were networking. You probably wanted to help, you just couldn't.

But as layoffs have become more common, this attitude is becoming less and less common. People realize it could happen to them. There's much less blaming of the unemployed person. Helping people in an unemployed situation is becoming more prevalent.

If you read the newspapers or catch the daily news on TV or radio, employed people are beginning to realize that unemployment for them might be closer than it has ever been in the past. Thus, they are more inclined to help than ever before.

Making Contacts

How do you make the contacts?

There are a variety of ways.

First, there is the trusty telephone. Where would we be without it, especially the cell phone? Although this is still the most common means of making contact, it can be difficult at times.

If you're attempting to make contact with a senior-level executive, you might have to be screened by their executive or administrative assistant. This can be a difficult situation, but it is one you will have to deal with.

If an assistant does not answer, you might be directed directly to voice mail. This can be traumatic, but it is only a minor roadblock. If you get the executive assistant, try to get them to be an ally of yours. Be as friendly and delightful as possible.

When they ask what the call is in reference to and you have a referral from your networking, immediately use that referral by stating something like "Mr. Freeman (the person who referred you), an acquaintance of mine and also of Mr. Big Cheese, suggested I arrange a meeting with Mr. Big Cheese in order to discuss industry opportunities." Be as succinct as possible and try not to spend a lot of time elaborating. It's not necessary. Hopefully the assistant will understand the circumstances, and since you did get a referral, she will put you through to Mr. Cheese or send you to voice mail or, if she is the keeper of the calendar, set up the meeting for you. All three alternatives are possible, so be prepared for each one.

If the person you're trying to meet (Mr. Cheese) does answer, explain to him that Mr. Freeman suggested you call him in order to arrange a visit to discuss how Mr. Cheese might be able to assist you in exploring new business opportunities.

Since Mr. Cheese probably has had calls like this in the past, he will quickly realize what the purpose is, and if he is in a helping mood, may arrange to visit with you. If he thinks you're just looking for a job and there are none at his firm, he might not want to visit with you at all. If that's the case, thank him for his time and move on. In my experience it is not wise to make up some sort of bogus excuse to get the meeting if there is no initial positive response.

If Mr. Cheese asks you directly if you're searching for a job, say you are, but not necessarily at his corporation, even though you really might be. Tell him you want the best fit. By responding that way, you're taking the pressure off.

If there is no opportunity within his firm, this can help put him at ease. Just try and arrange the meeting. What you'll discuss in the meeting will be covered later.

If you're directed to his voice mail you must be ready with a very precise statement as to what you want. First, make certain you mention your referral, then state you would like to arrange a meeting with him to discuss new business opportunities.

Again, short and to the point is the way to go. Do not leave a long message, don't elaborate. Make sure you leave your phone number (twice – speak slowly); if possible give him a time when you know you will be by the phone to answer it. This is important so that telephone tag is not played too often. Obviously, if you have a cell phone leave that number, too.

If the assistant keeps Mr. Cheese's calendar, you might be in luck. Be as nice and easygoing as possible. Mention your referral, explain your circumstances to the assistant, and ask to be placed on Mr. Cheese's calendar.

Try not to schedule more than twenty minutes for this meeting. It shows you have respect for his time. Thank her and tell her that you look forward to meeting her and Mr. Cheese. Hang up.

The Cold Call (brrrrrrrrrrrrrrrrrrrrrrrrrrrr)

Another telephone method you could use is the "cold call" – telephoning a person without any referral. However, even for professional sales people this can be very difficult.

It is not an easy thing to do. You must practice first so you don't come across unprepared. If you do make cold calls, the best thing that can happen is that the contact answers the phone himself and you can get right to your purpose.

Since the person doesn't know you or anything about you, this can be very difficult and stressful, but if you're adept in communication, give it a try. If you get a meeting, you're ahead of the game.

(Personally, I have no experience with "cold e-mails." But if you can keep it from seeming like spam, try it.)

Remember, *the only objective of these telephone scenarios is to set up a meeting*. The meetings are absolutely crucial in moving forward and getting a new job or opportunity. How crucial? There is nothing more important.

Here's an extremely valuable lesson I learned over the years: If you're looking for a new opportunity or searching for new business clients, no one or almost no one will hire you or buy your product or service or do anything with you unless they've met you in person. So the only objective of these telephone conversations is to arrange a meeting in person, face-to-face.

The second method of making contact is via a letter followed up with a phone call.

Experts believe the letter/phone method is the best way to arrange a meeting. It is a pretty good method, especially if you do not know the person or have not been referred to him. This method is time consuming, but don't rule it out. Again, the major objective is to arrange a meeting, regardless of the approach.

How does the letter method work? If you're trying to arrange a meeting with a person in a targeted company, write a letter to that person explaining that you're exploring ways to get into that industry. Since he or she has been successful, you would like to arrange a meeting to discuss how to succesfully enter their industry.

Basically, you would like expert advice. Like the phone call, try not to admit you're specifically looking for a job. You don't have to be real vague, but if you can, at least be slightly evasive.

The main reason you try not to come out and say you're looking for a job is that it puts too much pressure on the person you're hoping to meet. If their company does not have a job, in many cases they feel awkward about having you come in knowing that your purpose cannot be met by them.

(This strategy usually works with senior-level executives, who believe they are experts and, in many cases, might be. Junior-level or lower-level executives know at this point in time they are not experts and thus they believe if you come in for a meeting you're only trying to take their jobs. They probably won't take the time to visit with you.)

Remember to keep track of the date you mailed the letter so you know when to follow up. One other thing, do not send out hundreds of these letters at one time. Keep it to a manageable number, maybe five or ten, because rarely will the executive or his or her administrative assistant call you up to arrange that meeting.

That follow up is something you absolutely have to do. If you mail out a large number of letters, you will not be able to track all of them on a timely basis. It's a huge negative not to follow up when you said you would.

Even if you have a great computer program that can keep track of all the letters and names, the difficulty arises when you have to make the follow-up calls. These take time, so be patient with the number sent out.

In your letter, you must inform the person to whom you're writing that you will follow up with a phone call next week to arrange a meeting if you don't hear from him. If you send a pile of letters out, you won't be able to track them all. That's bad. Send five to ten and follow up. That's good.

Another tip. When you tell the person you will follow up via the phone, don't name a specific date – give yourself a week's latitude. For example, don't say you will call on October 5. Instead, say you will call during the week of October 5.

You do this because if you get busy and cannot return the call when you promise, again that's a negative. If you say "the week of…" you have a five-day period of time that can take into consideration any unscheduled meetings, out of town trips, etc.

There is one twist to this letter writing and advanced notice of your call back. The executive will know you'll be calling, and if for some reason he doesn't want to meet with you, he can inform his assistant of this fact, and she will do what is required to keep you from contacting him. That's OK.

If someone doesn't want to meet, what kind of meeting would it have been? You're both better off. Move on. If one letter in five (with follow up) works, that's a good result. One in ten is OK. If it's less than that, you need to reexamine both your letter and who you're contacting.

During this letter writing and phone call phase, making contact can be difficult.

Since people do have jobs, networking meetings are usually low on their priority list. Setting up a meeting might take you several weeks. Don't be discouraged. This is quite normal.

If you've written five to ten letters, the follow-up process can keep you busy. And you have to keep sending out more letters, because when searching for a new opportunity, it can come down to a numbers exercise – the more you send out, the better it is. But it must be controllable.

One other point. If you do know someone who knows the executive you're trying to reach, mention them within the first sentence or two of your letter. That referral can compress the time line and get you in quicker. When you call you might get the executive assistant or voice mail. Be prepared to explain your purpose in a very concise manner. Remember, you're only trying to arrange a meeting, nothing more at this time. Do not go into a big elaborate story. Now is not the time.

All of this will take time. It takes time to write the letter, mail the letter, and place the follow-up telephone calls the next week. And who knows how long it will take to arrange the actual meeting once the follow-up calls have been placed.

It takes a minimum of one week to ensure the letter you mailed reaches the subject. If you place the initial call and you don't talk to your subject, you cannot keep calling back daily. It is my recommendation that once the initial call is made you wait one week to make a second follow-up call. This shows you're persistent but not a nag.

That is critical because the meeting is being set up to help you, not help the person you're trying to meet.

As stated earlier, it will be rare that contacts will call you back immediately. Remember, they are busy and you're not a high priority.

(Even when I'm on a company's payroll engaged in a consulting assignment, it still might take several calls on my part to get through to the person I'm trying to meet – and they're paying me. Just imagine what it's like when you're just trying to get a meeting. Be patient.)

The "e" Option

The third way of making contact is via e-mail.

More and more people are doing business via e-mail. You might wonder if it would be more convenient to network and set up meetings by e-mail instead of telephone.

Preferences vary. But we are finding that more and more busy executives prefer e-mail. If the telephone seems not to be working, try the "e" road.

This is a great method because even if you can't get in touch with the person via the letter or phone method, e-mail usually gets a quick response. If I've tried to contact someone via phone and it has been several days and they've not returned my call, I will e-mail them – and usually within a day or less I get a reply.

E-mail has replaced almost all other communication devices. That's great when searching for a new opportunity. E-mail is almost the most effective and quickest because most executives access their own e-mail and read it.

Rarely does it get screened by an executive assistant like letters or telephone calls. And with new technology, even if executives travel a lot, they can still access their e-mail on the road. Thus during downtimes they use their e-mail as the main communication tool. You can readily arrange a meeting with them using this approach.

The difficulty with e-mail is that, since it has become so accessible, executives guard it pretty closely. If you can get their business cards, it usually contains their e-mail address with all their other pertinent information.

If you don't have that card, their e-mail address can be difficult to obtain. So how can you get an e-mail address of the person you desire?

I'm not a computer expert, but I have found that if you can get the e-mail address of anyone in the targeted company, usually the e-mail address of each employee is a simple derivative of that e-mail address. Thus, usually finding out one person's e-mail address can lead to others within the same organization. (Pretty cool, huh?)

For example, if you know that Jane Levett's e-mail address is jane.levett@thecompany.com and you want to reach Fred Schultz at the same company, chances are his e-mail address is fred.schultz@thecompany.com. In some instances it might be different, but normally this example applies.

In other instances, executives are listed on the company's website and e-mail addresses might be listed there, too.

The fourth way of making contact is through some outside social event, normally unrelated to a current business situation.

This can either be a meeting at an outside social function, like a wedding, bar mitzvah, birthday party, nonprofit fundraiser, or a similar event. These accidental meetings can be very rewarding.

(If you remember the scene from *Working Girl*, Melanie Griffith and Harrison Ford hooked up with an investment broker at his daughter's wedding and were able to arrange a meeting with him for a future radio station buyout.)

Contacts made this way can be very productive (though I don't recommend sneaking into a wedding uninvited). If you and your spouse are invited to a wedding or some other social function, this is a great place to make contacts. I've made a number of contacts at functions like these. If you're sitting with a group at a table and you don't know some of the attendees, make conversation with them.

Don't just gravitate to the people you know. The ones you don't know might hold the key to a new opportunity. Visit other tables where you might know one or two people and introduce yourself to the others. Strike up conversations with them. Don't be embarrassed.

Now, don't go talking to them about the fact that you're unemployed and you would like them to hire you. Just make some innocent conversation so you can find out what they do.

If it is something that can help you, ask them for a business card or some contact information and then ask them if you can call them the following week.

You'd like to arrange a meeting with them. Don't be very specific at the social function, but if you hit it off with them, they'll be accommodating. As I said in the prelude, "opportunities come in the strangest guises." Don't overlook any.

I was recently at a wedding and sitting at the table was a couple I didn't know. We began talking, and the next thing you know, we exchanged business cards. (By the way, always carry some sort of business card with you.) I called him the following week and we arranged a meeting to discuss how I might be able to help his business grow.

Another productive way of making contact is through some type of business luncheon or gathering.

If you know someone affiliated with a group, ask them to invite you to a meeting. Again, they can be very productive.

Usually before the luncheon or the speaker's presentation there is some type of social gathering. It might be a cocktail hour or just a plain old networking opportunity. Prepare to

mingle and try to pick out people who you don't know. As in a social function, it is not good to gravitate to people you already know. They can help with introductions, but it is good to move to people you don't know as soon as feasible.

At these events, continually be alert. You're probably not the only person trying to arrange meetings.

There is a good chance other people searching for opportunities are also in the audience. Although they might be a source of contacts, don't hang around with them. They are the competition. Mingle and make contact with people who can arrange meetings and help you find a new opportunity.

If you end up with a group of people who are mainly in transition, your chance of arranging productive meetings are lessened.

(Remember the fraternity rush scene in the movie *National Lampoon's Animal House*? All the losers sat on one couch and no matter what Pinto and Flounder did to mingle with the mainstream guests, they were always escorted back to the couch. Make sure you're not mingling with the "couch people.")

Another way of making contact is to be a member of a business or nonprofit organization, like the Rotary Club, or Chamber of Commerce, or religious organizations.

These organizations meet weekly or monthly. If you've been actively involved, this is a great place to continue your networking and get referred to individuals you haven't met during the meetings before your bout with unemployment.

These organizations are a great way to give back to the community, and that is always a positive sign. Individuals who are affiliated with these types of organizations have great contacts and are willing to help those who help others.

Even though there might be a yearly membership fee or contribution, it is definitely worthwhile. You're not only helping the organization, you're helping yourself.

Another great way to make contacts in a nonbusiness environment is at your children's sporting events – their soccer, baseball, football, swimming, and basketball games.

Regardless of what the sport is, this is a great way for parents to meet, socialize, and network.

Of course, this might be difficult if you (1) have no children; (2) have children, but they don't participate in sports; (3) have young children who aren't old enough to play; or (4) have older children who have moved out of the house.

If any of these circumstances are prevalent, you can still attend as a friend or neighbor or as a grandparent, if that applies. Since many business executives have children and since most tend to get involved in their children's extracurricular activities, this is a fantastic way to meet people in a nonthreatening environment.

Another way to meet people for contacts is getting yourself a part-time job.

Getting a part-time job helps in several ways.

First, it provides a paycheck. This can only be positive.

Second, a part time job gets you off of the couch, out of the house, and back in the working world.

It's amazing how a low-paying, part-time job can improve your outlook on life and motivate you to find more meaningful work. Having a chunk of your day set aside for work also somehow makes it easier and less painful to find the time to revise that résumé, send out those cover letters, and nail down those networking meetings.

Any high school physics student knows it takes less energy to keep a moving object moving than to start a still object into motion.

So keep moving.

Third, it can put you in contact with people who might be hiring. Now, don't just get any job. Try and get one that will put you in contact with the "right people." For example, what about a sales position at an exclusive men's or women's apparel store.

It can be a department store like Macy's, Bloomingdales, or Neiman Marcus, if they are available. Are you handy? Try a

Lowe's or Home Depot. My publishers met a guy with publishing sales experience while furnishing their new offices. It can be a sporting goods store, a jewelry store, or some other place where executives or their spouses shop.

These are great places to meet influential people, and if you're working nights and weekends you will meet some very interesting clientele.

These jobs are usually available during the holiday season and can lead to other, more exciting opportunities.

You might think these types of jobs will get in the way of your opportunity searches, but if you work nights and on weekends, there shouldn't be a problem.

A very important note…getting a full-time job is a full-time job. You must spend as much time as possible in your opportunity search.

If you think hard enough, you can probably come up with other venues to make contacts. That's great. The key here is to not overlook anything or anyone.

If you believe for any reason the opportunity or contact might be too remote, forget about your doubts and try anyway.

There are a lot of unemployed people out there not willing to take risks. They will only contact their friends, relatives, neighbors, and maybe past employers. These type of contacts are all necessary.

However, you will benefit from more contacts. It will be necessary to develop relationships with total strangers to improve your chances of finding that new opportunity.

For some of you this can be very difficult and even threatening. It is not easy for many people to make contact with strangers and arrange meetings to expand their networks. But it must be done. The rewards are many.

A Once in a Lifetime Offer

Since meeting people can be a problem for some, that's why, ladies and gentlemen, I am offering you an exciting new correspondence course on how to meet strangers and set up meetings to further your networking capabilities.

It's titled "How to Meet Strangers and Set up Meetings to Further Your Networking Capabilities." Pretty catchy, huh?

Here's What You'll Learn

- Learn how not to accept no for an answer (a double negative?)
- Learn the techniques of going around the administrative assistant in order to meet the appropriate "Mr. Cheese" and other influential people
- Explore the ways you ask for a job without asking for a job
- See actual demonstrations via videotape on how to arrange and hold a meeting for hours
- Review actual case studies from individuals who receive great sums of money without performing any worthwhile tasks (politicians, evangelists, consultants, etc.)
- Through actual role playing in the privacy of your own home, if you still have one, you will actually practice from pre-edited scripts all the techniques you need to "make the contact."

Don't be left out of the loop.

Become a part of one of the most rapidly growing segments in the American economy – unemployment.

While you're unemployed, don't just sit around wishing and hoping it wasn't happening to you, go out and better yourself. This course is the way to do just that. For a nominal fee of $595 you learn how to make it happen in your own abode. Don't be shy. Don't be embarrassed, and, most importantly, don't be cheap. Send your money to our educational institute today.

Act now! Remember, for every day that goes by, another opportunity goes by with it.

Send your money to:

The Ineedabuck Institute

52 Borrowed Money Lane

West Palm Beach, Florida 30303

Don't forget to take advantage of our "Delighted Guarantee."

If after reviewing the material you're not completely delighted, just send it back to us. We won't refund your money, but we will be delighted for you – absolutely free.

Pardon me, sometimes I get sidetracked.

Now, just because you've been successful in making the contacts doesn't mean you've completed your task. There is still a lot you have to do. What do you think would be the next logical step? How about setting up the meeting? Good idea.

The Next Step in Networking...

The next step in networking is setting up the meeting.

Since you've already made contact, setting up the meeting will be a breeze, right? Wrong. In some cases, this can be the toughest part, aside from getting an actual job offer.

Setting up a meeting entails a tremendous amount of fortitude, endurance, creativity, and just plain patience. Just because you've made contact does not mean a meeting is forthcoming.

In general, you really don't want to come out and say the reason you want to meet with Mr. Big Guy is to see if he has a job for you. You really need to come up with another reason – a good one.

This is my recommendation, even if the company is hiring. Here's an example why.

Let's say you notice through your research that the company does have a job opening and you mention it to get the meeting with Mr. Big Guy. Chances are he'll refer you directly to the human resources department. That's why, even if you know the company has an opening, I believe it's advisable not to mention it when arranging the meeting.

After all, he will know of the opening, and if you make a good impression, he'll mention the opening to you.

If he doesn't mention it to you and the meeting is about to end, you might want to bring it up tactfully to see if he can suggest a channel for you to inquire about the job opening formally. Heck, he might even recommend you to the appropriate department if your meeting went well.

You should not mention that you're actively seeking a position with the company because you must be able to put the executive, or the person you're meeting with, at ease.

This takes the pressure off that person, and he does not have to be defensive if an opening does not exist.

Later on we'll discuss how to act in the actual meeting, but for now we're only interested in setting up the meeting.

If you're able to drop a name as a referral, such as, "Mr. Big Guy, Fred Smith suggested I meet with you," a meeting is more probable, especially if Mr. Big Guy knows Fred. Mention Fred's name as quickly as possible so as to put Mr. Big Guy at ease, but always remember to be professional.

In some cases the person you're trying to meet will ask you how you know Fred. Be honest. If you met Fred during a networking meeting a couple of days ago, let it be known that's how you met him. People network all of the time. It's not strange that a person you just met will refer you to others. However, be sure that you actually do have that referral.

When networking you must always ask the person who is doing the referring if you can use his or her name. If, for some reason, the person says no, don't use it.

If they qualify their referral, respect that qualification. Misusing a name will come back to haunt you in the future.

If you can use humor wisely, go ahead. But be careful, it's not for everyone. Using humor can be a tightrope to travel. If you're not totally comfortable with using humor, don't. But by all means, be pleasant and upbeat. People prefer to meet pleasant people.

If the people you're trying to meet have searched for jobs in the past, they should have some compassion for you and will be happy to assist you.

Some of the best meetings you will attend are with people who just got hired.

In this case, "been there, done that" is a good thing.

Not every meeting will be a good one. Some of the worst meetings you might encounter will probably be with people who, for some reason, have either worked for one company all of their lives or who have never been laid off. Some of these people have no idea what it's like to search for a new opportunity and might not be very helpful. Too bad. However, if you can arrange a meeting with them, you must pursue it.

You never know when that network connection will pay off. Keep plugging. All it takes is one helpful lead, and you never can tell where that lead will come from.

Another way to arrange a meeting is to have someone arrange it for you.

This can be truly rewarding. If you know a senior executive, or for that matter anyone who knows someone at a company, and they will call on your behalf, that's great.

Not only will you get that meeting, but in many cases, the person who did the calling might accompany you to the meeting. For example, this meeting might be in the form of a luncheon, which can be a terrific way to meet. Hey, it might even be a free meal. Then again, since they're doing you the favor it might be on you.

Oops. You show up but no one's there.

Having acquaintances set up meetings is great. But it's not a perfect world. What happens if a meeting is arranged and the person you plan to meet with cancels the meeting? Or better still, what if you show up and he forgot to cancel the meeting and he's not there but you are?

Well, this can happen – and you need to stay positive.

If he calls to cancel or his administrative assistant calls, more than likely they will apologize and do everything possible to reschedule the meeting. Once this occurs and the meeting does take place, the person will do everything he or she can to be helpful.

As we said, it's not a perfect world. You're trying to arrange meetings in a quick and efficient manner to get a new opportunity. Any delay puts your time table back, maybe as long as a couple of weeks. The road from hell to hallelujah can be a long one. However, there's not much you can do about it. Accept it and move forward.

An Alternative Oops

Another alternative is you have a meeting scheduled, and no one calls you to cancel, and you show up at the office and he is gone, usually out of town.

This can occur because, as mentioned earlier, you're not a top priority.

The administrative assistant will come out and apologize as much as possible. You must remain calm and be professional. Remember that pleasant, upbeat thing – but don't act like it doesn't matter. You can be a little unhappy, but don't be angry. Explain how you know these situations can occur. And ask immediately to reschedule the appointment.

Try not to leave without another appointment set up. In many cases when the person you were to meet with finds out what happened, you will get a call from that person, also apologizing. And that person will try to make sure to be there next time. If you were not able to schedule a follow-up appointment, this is the time to do it. Remember, with all the downsizing that's gone on, a lot of people are too busy. Hmmm. Maybe they need help.

Setting up the actual appointments calls for a great deal of patience and endurance.

First, it might take you several weeks just to talk with the person you're trying to meet.

Second, since you're low on the priority list – or not on the list at all – pretty much everything comes before you and the meeting. Deal with it. Stay upbeat.

So continue to have the endurance of a hungry lion.

Keep calling. Over and over again. You might think you're being an imposition, and in some cases you might. But keep on calling and arranging those meetings.

Always be persistent, it's a great trait to have.

When to Stop.

Now, there may come a point where you might decide the effort is greater then the reward. If the person you're trying to meet continues to put you off or refuses to talk with you, even on the phone, well, get a clue. Move on.

And don't take it personally – even if your feelings are hurt.

It's just life in the U-Zone. It's not worth getting upset over this all-too-common scenario. You've got enough to worry about without adding to the list.

A useful tip to those employed. If people are trying to set up networking meetings with you, be courteous and try to schedule some of them. If you can't, try to be helpful as you say no.

I understand you might be busy, but there are times when you can really help someone.

You can't spend all day, everyday in networking meetings, but once in a while meet someone who is networking.

You can develop a short list of things you can do to help. Some day they might be able to help you.

You've now been extremely fortunate and have arranged several networking meetings. You sit back and enjoy your success and think, "This isn't so bad."

You keep thinking, "Now that I've arranged a few meetings, once these people see me and my qualifications the offers will be rolling in. The only decision I'll have to make is how much money I should settle for."

As they say, "Dream on."

Trust me. No matter how hard you try to not let this happen, these thoughts will enter your mind.

You will convince yourself that you're better than the rest of the people looking for a new opportunity. You should be positive, you should stay upbeat. But you have to realize that the odds of quickly getting a new opportunity are slim.

If you're fortunate enough to arrange a lot of meetings in a short period of time, you really will be convinced that a new opportunity is just around the corner.

Don't be misled. It probably won't happen. Because although arranging meetings is a necessary step, remember one thing is true…

Meetings Aren't Jobs

Meetings will not and cannot pay the bills.

Meetings are just that… meetings.

A meeting might lead to a job, but in the majority of cases, meetings will lead to other meetings.

And that's OK.

Because without these meetings you probably won't find that next business opportunity.

So do everything you can to arrange these meetings. They have other advantages. First, believe it or not, they can keep you from losing your mind. Because setting up meetings accomplishes a number of things

First, meetings get you out of your house. Even with *Jerry Springer*, *Montel*, *Jeopardy*, *The Pyramid*, *Oprah*, etc., being at home can be a very boring situation.

There's only so much ESPN you can watch. As a former Chicagoan, I had to deal with the fact that not all Cubs game are televised nationally on WGN anymore during the daytime.

If you're home alone, it can drive you nuts. If you're at home with a spouse, that can drive you nuts. Arrange a meeting.

Second, a meeting will also give your brain something to think about.

You just don't walk into a meeting without doing some background research about the company and the environment it operates in.

It might just be a meeting, but it could turn into a job.

If you come prepared for a meeting, and during the conversation you impress the person with your knowledge of the company and industry, if you ask the right questions, he might ask you to return to further discuss the opportunities or connect you with someone else in the industry. There might even be a part-time consulting project. If you're meeting with decision makers and there is no available position, they may be so impressed with you that a position is created for you. Many company positions are found in this manner.

Do some research. The meeting you have today might be the job you have tomorrow.

Third, a meeting is a forum to meet people you never would have met if you weren't searching for a new opportunity.

Today, people are usually too engrossed with their jobs to find the time to meet the people they might find interesting or even enjoyable.

These days, meeting new interesting people can be hard as people keep their noses to the grindstone and work to survive in a tight economy.

Keep in mind that these meetings may benefit the people you meet with by increasing their circle of contacts and their sphere of influence.

It can be a win-win situation for everyone.

Fourth, setting up meetings will also keep you occupied instead of looking at the clock or wondering why you haven't found the next opportunity. Meetings make the days go by more quickly. This can be critical for your own sanity. There's nothing worse than sitting around the house all day with nothing to do. There are only so many faucet leaks to fix, rooms to paint, light bulbs to change, hedges to trim, and groceries to shop for.

Meetings will keep you occupied in a couple of ways. You have to get in your car and drive to them. This can take some time. Next you will wait in the reception area, could be as long as half an hour. Again, you're not the top priority and you may have to wait.

Hey, what else do you have to do? If there is someone else in the reception area, strike up a conversation. Who knows, it might lead to a job lead or another meeting. Now is not the time to be timid.

Then there is the meeting itself. This can last anywhere from a half-hour to a couple of hours. I mean it. Some of these meetings can last a long time if there is a positive connect. They can be fun and very informative.

Next you get to drive back to your house. Finally, there is the thank you letter or e-mail, the follow up that must take place, thanking the person for their time, input, information, other leads, etc., and maybe a lunch.

So, when you add it all up, the meeting plus the follow up can take most of the day from beginning to the end.

Well, there's your day. Where did the time go? Like I say, in some cases one meeting might take up the entire day. When scheduling meetings, make sure you account for these time frames so you can prepare accordingly.

You can never have too many meetings. If you can set up two meetings per day, that can really keep you occupied, and it will enhance your chances of finding the right opportunity.

After all, that's what it's all about.

Also, there is no such thing as a useless meeting. They might not all be productive, but they're not useless.

One interesting thing about these people and meetings is that **you will never know in advance which ones will be good and which ones will not be so productive**.

Thus, every meeting is important.

The person who you believe will be a waste of time will turn out to be the most productive and vice versa.

Finally, and most importantly, setting up a meeting can actually lead to a new, exciting job opportunity. You have to make meetings to create opportunities.

Be Careful of Meetings

You might get to the point where you measure your success based on the number of meetings you schedule. Don't be fooled. Although meetings are important, they don't pay the rent.

When I was searching for that new opportunity, my wife would ask me how it was going.

I'd respond by saying, "Oh, just great! I had two meetings today and set up three more."

And it's true. It is progress.

You're not there yet. But you're getting there.

Now comes the next step…the actual meeting itself.

How do you act? It's not enough to set up a meeting. At that meeting you must be able to present yourself in a dignified manner, a person who can contribute to the organization. If you haven't done this for a while, it can be nerve-racking.

You just can't walk in, talk constantly about yourself, and expect to make a favorable impression. Many people think a meeting is good when they do most of the talking. **The key to a successful meeting is to get the other person to do a lot of the talking.** It's like selling. Most great salespeople go into a meeting and begin to ask questions, getting the other person to talk while they listen intently. That's how you learn what is needed – so you can fulfill those needs.

Think about it – if you can get the other person to do a good share of the talking and some time goes by, one of the main things they will remember is that you were a friendly, understanding individual who had a business outlook similar to their own. They may forget they did most of the talking and form a good impression about you.

If you ask appropriate questions, they will ramble on about what they know best, their business and themselves.

This can provide more information for future discussions.

So, tip number one is do *not* monopolize the conversation.

Don't be mute, but try to get your contact to do most of the talking. Of course, introduce yourself and work in your background and accomplishments, but after that, try to make it a meeting, not a monologue.

Try to get him or her going. Find out as much as you can about the person and the organization.

The more you know and the more involved you become, the more you will be involved in a situation that can lead to an offer or a project or another lead.

What You Should Look For

Here are some of the topics that can make your meeting.

Try and find out if your contact is happy with the company's performance. If not, what is the problem? Monopolizing a conversation normally turns people off, and that's the last thing you want to do since it probably took you a long time to arrange the meeting in the first place. During the meeting drop hints as to how you might be able to assist the organization.

Remember, you've mentioned you're not expecting an opportunity within the company. However if there was an opportunity, you would want to be considered as a candidate.

When you begin one of these networking meetings you might notice something right off the bat. You probably won't be as nervous as if you were going on a "real" job interview.

Why is that, you might ask? The main reason is that there is no undue pressure on any of the participants.

Since you're not interviewing for an actual position, you and your contact can relax and be at ease.

He's not interviewing you for a job opening, and since there might not be any job available, you aren't interviewing, either.

You can joke, if you're comfortable doing so, talk about all kinds of subjects, and relate past experiences that might even have been failures. Depending on his or her comfort level and how he or she views you (are you a peer, are you similar in age, is your experience level close?), your contact might take the opportunity to discuss many subjects other than work, because this kind of meeting is a nonthreatening situation.

Once the pressure is off, a meeting usually goes pretty well. Your contact sees you in an environment more like an outside-of-the-office experience.

If the impression is a good one, you may end up developing a long-lasting acquaintanceship. This can be very beneficial in the long term even though you want a job in the short term. Don't let short-term objectives pressure you so much that you can't enjoy this part of your life – or this particular meeting.

Even though you're undergoing a negative experience, there are positive things occurring. You're building your network. Step back once in a while and appreciate what you're doing.

One of the positive things about your current unemployed position is these meetings and contacts. They are a resource that can pay off in both new career opportunities and new friendships. You'll see.

OK, back to the actual meeting. Since there is no longer any pressure for you to perform well, you will. I think it's one of Murphy's Laws – "If you don't need to perform well, you will." But, you might have to wait a bit...

While You're Waiting

One of the first things you will encounter before the meeting is usually the administrative assistant. Be very friendly and go out of your way to make this person your ally. An assistant who is your ally can be a huge asset. They can grant easier access to the person you're meeting and expedite the occurance of future meetings. So be nice to the administrative assistant while you are waiting to meet your contact.

If you're waiting in the reception area, you might even strike up a conversation with the receptionist. In large offices she might be the one to screen calls, and in smaller offices she might be your person's administrative assistant. Getting these people on your side can only be advantageous. In fact, every person you meet will be an opportunity.

They Ask for Your Card and You Don't Have One

Hold it. You must *always* have a business card – even if it was just made on your home computer. Never be without business cards that contain your personal contact information.

Today, business cards are relatively inexpensive, and many computer programs make it easy to print them yourself. Business cards are an absolutely vital marketing tool, and you should always have them handy – no matter what.

If a person you meet in the waiting room is employed, use the same networking skills that you'd use over the telephone. One advantage here is that you've already made personal contact.

If you can't set up a meeting right then and there, make sure to get a business card and follow up with a phone call at a later date. A meeting should follow.

This is networking in action.

If the person in the reception area is unemployed, it's still networking. That person might have contacts you don't and vice versa. Leave no stone unturned.

Unemployed individuals can be a great asset. They have empathy for other unemployed people and will usually go out of their way to assist you. Their networking base might be large so, if you can, arrange a meeting to compare notes. They might know of a situation you're not aware of, especially if they come from a different industry or discipline.

The Meeting

After waiting for what might seem an eternity you will finally be summoned to the office.

Depending on the stature of the person you're meeting, this office might be more impressive than your own home.

I've been in some offices where I could live.

It is certainly acceptable to make some positive comments on the office and its décor, if that's appropriate. The purpose of a networking meeting is to build your network.

Discuss how he can provide you with other networking individuals while at the same time determining if there is an opening within his organization that you might be able to fill.

In addition, if during your visit you realize that the company might have some sort of challenge in front of it that your contact is concerned about, and if you can show him that you might be able to provide a solution to that challenge, don't be afraid to explore that avenue. That can be a very positive step in gaining his confidence for future meetings.

Since you're the one who arranged the meeting, you should be prepared to set the tone and direction.

However, if the person you're meeting wants to determine how it should go, let him. He might have a hidden agenda as to why the meeting was accepted, and you should allow him to proceed in any direction he wants to go.

Remember, body language tells its own story, too.

Always go into any meeting with a positive attitude, both mentally and physically. Enthusiasm and a positive attitude are two of the most powerful traits you can display in a networking meeting.

These two traits can be extremely contagious, so if you display them, your audience will display them, too. Even if you're about to enter your thirtieth meeting with no appreciable results, you must remain enthusiastic and positive.

For a start, don't sing the blues. Few people who are employed are interested in your unemployment problems. It makes them sad and uncomfortable. Don't be negative.

If you start lambasting your former coworker, boss, salary, work hours, time traveling, etc., you will have turned off the person you're meeting with and you won't get assistance.

No matter how sad or angry you might be, remain positive. I remember in one interview I was asked about five different ways how I felt about a former employer.

Each time the question was asked I responded in a positive manner, not really knowing what the interviewer was trying to accomplish.

After the interview was over, he complimented me on the way I handled the questions. He was trying to see if I would say negative things about that employer. I never did, and later I got the job. Being positive throughout the session was one of the things that helped.

Interviewers have ways of disguising questions to seek certain responses. Make sure you don't fall into that trap. Stay optimistic. So let a smile be your umbrella and enter that meeting enthusiastic and upbeat. Make it easy for the person you're meeting to help a nice person like you.

The Meeting Continues...

You'll notice that a networking meeting can be very different from a job interview. First, you can relax a little.

Since you're going into this meeting without any job or opportunity expectations, you don't put undue pressure on yourself. Even though you're looking for a job opportunity, and may be under a good bit of pressure, do not expect too much from an initial networking meeting. If you do, you will be disappointed.

We talked earlier about unrealistic expectations. Assuming you're going to land a job in this first meeting is a good example. So lighten up and enjoy the moment.

You'll be meeting with people you probably never would have met if the circumstances were different. This is a good thing. Take a deep breath, relax, and make the most of this situation.

If you haven't spent a great deal of time meeting strangers, it's important during this initial meeting to try and put them at ease. They might be uncomfortable. Don't look like a person who is unemployed for the past year. Present yourself in a positive light and get them to start talking about themselves and where they see opportunities.

Obviously, if you have a mutual acquaintance, you can start by talking about him or her. This is the common thread between the two of you.

If you're a good conversationalist, the meeting will progress in a smooth manner. If you aren't, practice what you want to cover at home.

But remember, this is a discussion, not a speech.

In most cases, time will really fly by. However, keep a close eye on that time. If you know the person you're meeting has allocated only a half-hour, don't take longer for the meeting. If the person seems to want to extend the meeting, that's his call, but don't overstay your welcome. You want to show you respect your contact's time constraints.

If you haven't covered everything you wanted to during the time allotted, ask if you can schedule a follow-up meeting, or send a follow-up e-mail, or even invite that person to lunch.

If the meeting went well, that follow-up meeting might be scheduled right then and there. This is a good sign.

When I meet with a prospective client for the first time, I always try and arrange a follow-up visit. I usually ask, "What should the next steps be?" If they're not sure or hesitate, then I'll suggest the next step. This usually is another meeting. They usually agree. But you better have something to bring to that next meeting.

Once the meeting begins you'll be amazed at how much information you'll learn about the person and the company.

Try to ask some thought-provoking questions. But remember, if these questions are too deep, either about the person or the company, you might get a negative reaction. You must be aware.

And cautious.

My rule of thumb is to think of the person as a friend, but not a close friend. Someone you see once in a while.

By acting in this way, you won't be offensive and you will hopefully leave having made a good positive impression.

Show some initiative by researching the company. This is easy to accomplish using the Internet. You'll be amazed at what you can find out via the Internet.

Then discuss this research during the meeting. This research can go a long way towards helping your contact form a positive impression of you.

If you can talk intelligently about the company or the company's industry, you'll be remembered after the meeting. That is all you can expect.

You now know how to act in a networking meeting. By the way, if you act the same way when you encounter an actual job interview, you will also make a very favorable impression of yourself. Who knows, it could be the deciding factor in getting a job offer.

What You Should *Not* Do in a Networking Meeting

First, *do not* monopolize the conversation.

I talked about this before, but it needs to be repeated.

If you start to talk and never stop, there's a good chance that the person you're meeting will not be very impressed with you and, as a result, might not take the time to assist you.

This kind of behavior can easily happen if you're nervous and begin to ramble without much thought. Here's a sample ramble:

"Hello, my name is Steve. I am very happy to meet you, and thank you for your time. Can you believe what those jerks at Amalgamated Rubber did to me? After fifteen years of loyal service, those people fired me. I was doing a great job, but my boss was a real nincompoop. He had no idea what was going on. I can't tell you how often I covered up for his mistakes. The company was in financial ruin for years. If it wasn't for me they would have gone out of business years ago.

I kept them alive. And they turn around and do this to me. I helped everyone do a better job. I single-handedly increased sales in my division, without any help from those idiots in marketing. I developed a great new product, but those dipsticks in production screwed up the process. Those morons caused a great product to fail. You can't blame me for that. It was their fault. Why are they still there, and I got fired? I don't understand. I was a model employee. I'll get even. One day I'll get a good job, and when they come to me for help, I'll laugh in their faces. Oh, by the way, I was wondering, do you have a job for me?"

This is a little over the top – well, maybe – but a nonstop ramble can ensure that you won't have a prayer of getting any type of assistance.

We discussed this briefly, too: people are put in an uncomfortable position if you ask them for something they cannot deliver.

In networking, you're asking for help, connections, and information. So, **second**, no matter how much you may want to work for a certain company, and even if you know there is an opening, *do not* come out and say it at a networking meeting. If you act well during the meeting and the person knows of the opening, they might mention it to you and introduce you to the appropriate decision maker(s). Let them take the initiative – not you.

Later, you might call back and say you heard there was an opening – could you get assistance setting up an interview? But, again, this is only appropriate if the meeting went well.

Third, *do not* tell the person you're meeting with that you can do a better job than anyone else who is currently working for the company.

The minute you start to degrade others, you place yourself in a huge hole. Even if you know for a fact that the employees are constant underperformers and that your knowledge and training and experience would put you at the top of the performance pile, don't do it. The person you're meeting with might have hired those employees, or worse yet, they may be relatives.

Fourth, *do not* be so overly complimentary that the person knows you're just shoveling him a pile of manure.

It's one thing to be complimentary and positive, it's another to pile it on too deep. Don't think this doesn't happen – it does. There is a fine line between a bit of honesty and too much bologna. Know where the line is and don't cross over.

Here's an example of what not to say:

"Hello, my name is Steve. It is a pleasure to meet such a legend in the industry. I can't tell you how long I have been trying to meet you. Of all the people in this industry, I consider you to be the person who has been the greatest influence in my life and career. I even named my first child after you."

It's one thing to compliment people on their successes, it's another thing to make them ill.

Now that you know how and how *not* to act in a networking meeting, the next question should be… what should be your goals in the meeting?

Your Five Goals

When going into a networking meeting, you should have at least five goals. No, the first goal is not getting a job.

The first goal: Make the person you're meeting with like you. This is not revolutionary thinking. You will not get a job, a new business opportunity, or anything else unless the person you're meeting with likes you.

Interviewing for a job is like dating. First, you meet the person. Second, you get acquainted. He or she will take some time determining your likes and dislikes and vice versa. Third, you will hopefully begin to feel comfortable in each other's presence. Fourth, both of you begin to feel at ease and begin to open up about your own attitudes and so on. If everything clicks, you go out on another date, and a relationship flourishes.

Well, it's no different in finding a job or new opportunity. First, you meet each other. Next, you have a little exploratory conversation, to see if you can get along.

If you're at ease with each other and the other members of the team, you probably will realize you have similar attitudes about employment. If this happens there is a chance they may offer you the job – or, if there simply is no job, a helpful referral to someone who might have a job or knows someone who does.

One thing I learned in the process is this: if the people you're interviewing with treat you poorly or with a lack of respect during the search process, this is probably the best you will ever be treated. They are trying to determine whether or not they want you as an employee. If they treat you poorly during the interview process or promise you something that, once the offer is presented, is missing, what makes you think it will get better once they hire you? It probably never will. You may take the job anyway. And you may hope for a better world – just don't expect it.

I know a large number of individuals who were treated with disdain during the interviewing process. They had to haggle over salary, benefits, vacation time, etc.

They were never happy during this process. However, they believed that once they became an employee, the situation would be better. Guess what? It wasn't.

If you're treated poorly when a company actually seeks to recruit you, what makes you think you will be treated better when they have you as an employee? They won't.

As a matter of fact, in going back and talking with these individuals, they stayed with the company that treated them poorly during the interview process, on average, no more than eight months. They got fed up and either quit or found another opportunity while employed.

So as I said, make the person you're meeting like you, and consider carefully how they treat you. This may not be a profound thought, but it is a profound truth.

The second goal: Subtly let them know that you would like to be considered for job opportunities with the company.

Finding out about a job opportunity may take some tact and effort, but if an opportunity exists, let them know you would be interested in that opportunity.

However, as mentioned earlier, don't blatantly ask for a job. There is nothing wrong with letting the person you're meeting with in on your goals. Say something like, "You know, I have several goals during a networking meeting. One is, if you know of an opportunity, I certainly would like you to determine if I'd be a good candidate for that position, whether it is within your company or with another." By mentioning another organization, you're putting them somewhat at ease, especially if there is nothing within their own company.

Try to introduce your goals near the end of the meeting, not the beginning. This can be an excellent way to summarize the meeting, signaling the end of the meeting. Summarizing your goals also gives your contact something to think about after you leave.

The third goal: Make it to your contact's "top-of-mind awareness."Awareness is a goal that most advertisers want to achieve. So do you. For example, if someone asks you "What's the best automobile?" you might say BMW. .
You were aware of the brand name, it was "top of mind."

That's where you want to be in the mind of the person you just met. If, after your meeting, someone calls him or her to ask if he or she knows of a good candidate for a position, or mentions an opportunity opening up, you want that person to think of you.

The fourth goal: Have your contact keep your résumé on top of their "active" pile of future candidates.

It gets back to top-of-mind awareness. The same holds true in finding a new opportunity and networking. Business executives (or for that matter, anyone) have a lot of priorities. If you can get them to keep your résumé on top of their desk, you have a greater chance of being referred to other people when a new opportunity occurs.

But references won't happen unless they like you. If they don't like you or aren't impressed with you, your résumé will hit the trash can as soon as you walk out the door.

Although you're not "officially searching for a job per se," always be prepared to leave a résumé with the person you're meeting. This will provide them with a method to reach you and give them all of the necessary details about you.

You can leave the résumé with them at the end of the meeting by saying something like, "Even though there might not be anything available at your company, I'd really appreciate it if you'd keep my résumé in case you hear of anything.... thanks."

The fifth goal: Have your contact furnish you with names of other acquaintances who might be helpful in your search.

You can then set up more meetings to continue the development of your networking system.

This is critical. Getting in to meet people can be a difficult process. Knowing who they are is very difficult. Referrals make it easier. Now you can call the new person and say that Mr. So-and-So referred you. That normally leads to additional meetings, and that's what networking is all about.

As mentioned before, most opportunities are found through an active networking process. And it may be that second, third, or fourth level of connection that pays off.

The more networking meetings you have, the greater the chances of landing the employment opportunity you want. Like selling, it's a numbers game.

Your goal is not to set up hundreds of meetings. Your goal is to find a new opportunity.

So there you have it, not only the longest stage in the process but also the most productive. Once you've reached this stage, good things should start to happen. Not only can networking help you find a job, it can keep you occupied so that every day you just don't stare at the clock on the wall. It can also help you when you do get that new opportunity, especially if you get a sales position and the product you represent may interest the dozens of people you met while networking.

Remember, while networking, keep your eye on the future. When the big day comes and you land an exciting new business opportunity, the networking you did in the past can help you with your job in the future.

When I decided to start my own business, many of the people I met during my networking stage eventually became clients.

I never would have met them if I didn't take the time to determine what I wanted to do with my life and start my networking journey. And don't forget to keep in touch with them. They can be great allies to you, and perhaps now you can be a great ally to them and help them if they need it.

So for the past several weeks or months you've been networking your rear off. When does it stop? It shouldn't. Never stop networking. In this day and age, you need to stay connected. And you need to keep it a positive connection – send an article of interest, a note, maybe even an appropriate card. Don't just get connected – stay connected.

And keep making those connections. They may take you to a new kind of business, a new city, or a new way of looking at your career, but one day it will happen. There will come that fateful day when you wake up one morning and realize that you in fact did make it happen.

It may be a phone call, a sucessful interview, a teaching certificate, a job you might not have been willing to take six months earlier, or an opportunity with a distant connection made through your diligent networking. All the networking and other tactics you performed have finally paid off.

The telephone rings, and it's someone who would actually like to talk with you. Your prayers have been answered. The choir begins to sing.

Stage Seven...
Hallelujah!!!!!!!!!!!!!!!!!!!!!!!!!!!!

*"If it is to be,
it is up to me."*

That's right...Hallelujah!

Like most things in life, it happens when you least expect it. The telephone rings, and it's the new opportunity you've been waiting for, possibly praying for.

Depending how long you've been unemployed, you literally can feel your heart in your throat. You would swear it was there because it is difficult to breathe. You pinch yourself, you're not dreaming. It is true. You have an offer. Hopefully, it's the one job you want. If it's not the exact job you want, at least it's a job. And you grab it. Gratefully.

Now, take a deeeeeeeeeeeeeeeeeeeeeeeeeep breath and accept the offer. Don't say, "Well, that's a nice opportunity. I'll need some time to evaluate all of my options, and I'll get back to you in a couple of days." What you need to say is, "Thank you, it is what I've been looking for, and I'm excited about the opportunity. I'll see you in the office on Monday." Now hang up the phone and let the festivities begin.

I understand that you may have been on the unemployment roll for quite some time, and maybe the offer you get is way below what you had hoped for – or even a position at a lower level than what you're used to. But it is an opportunity. And right now opportunities may be fewer than we all wish.

Pick up any newspaper and read that thousands of people are losing their jobs even when there's job growth. Sometimes you might have to take a couple of steps backward to take several steps forward, later on. The key in this day and age is getting the offer. Make the most of the situation, become a productive member of the employed society, and figure out later how you can make the best of this situation.

Many people are considered to be underemployed. By that I mean they have taken a lesser job or a lesser salary just to get back in the employment arena. That's OK.

Use that time to hone your skills, and if necessary keep up your networking while employed. There is nothing wrong with that. And, actually, job offers come more easily to those who are already working.

Although you must be loyal to the company that is employing you and giving you an opportunity, you also must be loyal to yourself. Let me provide a real life example.

A Dilemma!

Many years ago I was offered a position with a company in a relatively small town. Coming from a large city (Chicago), I think I had more people living in my apartment building than lived in the town. Anyway, there was no way I would ever move to that town, but it was a good offer.

I had a dilemma. What should I do? Take the offer, knowing I would never move, but tell the company I would and continue to search for another opportunity or not take the offer and try to survive as I had done in the past?

I decided to seek guidance from an acquaintance who was head of a human resource department for a major company. Here is a sampling of our discussion.

I asked, "Lisa, what should I do, take the job knowing I won't move or not take the job and continue my search?" Lisa said, "Steve, let's say you take the job, move to the town, and after several months, the company undergoes a reorganization. Let's say you're one of the people eliminated. Do you think they would care whether or not you just moved to the town?

If you were not a part of their plans, you would be let go, and it would be up to you to move out of town back to where you were, at your own expense, unless you were able to negotiate some sort of move payment clause in your contract, if you got a contract at all. Being loyal to a company is very important, but do not put their needs above your own. Take the job, continue to look, and if you find something better, resign and move on with your life."

I was shocked by this advice, especially since it came from a human resource professional. I did take the job.

I commuted by plane at my expense for five months until I found a better opportunity. I resigned and moved forward. During those five months, I was a very productive employee and gave that company my best. Interestingly, when I left they didn't blink an eye. They moved forward, too.

The reason I bring this up is that even though the position you might accept is slightly below what you were searching for, it is important to take the opportunity. Do the best you can! Give them full value – and more. But nobody said you had to stop searching.

Let the Festivities Begin

Now you've accepted the offer. What do you do first?

If you have a spouse, that's your first phone call. He or she has been behind you for all this time. They have lived and died with each meeting, each phone call, and, in some cases, each rejection.

Don't just call on the phone. Be a little creative. Get some flowers – or something that you know your spouse would like.

Next, get a card expressing your feelings. If you can't find one, write one yourself. Remember, this is a joyous, momentous occasion. You should memorialize it. Hopefully, it doesn't happen often. Then make some dinner reservations at a favorite restaurant. No cooking tonight. If money's been tight, use the credit card. Soon you'll be able to cover the expenses again – *you have a job*.

If you have children, they should be next on the list. They've also suffered, and depending on their ages, may have suffered more than you. It's time to do something special for them. Be creative. Give them something out of the ordinary – and, as always, don't forget to give them plenty of your time and appreciation.

Make sure everyone remembers this day. It's one to be celebrated. Also make sure that you don't forget what it has been like for the past several months. It must be a learning experience for all – and in this economy, that new job may not last forever.

After those couple of calls, it's up for grabs and up to you. Parents, brothers and sisters, and friends that stuck by you when things might not have been looking so good. The supporting cast that kept you sane while going through this period of gloom. Select the one who's really helped you and take them out to dinner, too. Show them that you really care. I believe this is very important. There were those who were willing to stand by you when things were not so good – you should be willing to show your appreciation when things begin to get better.

Getting Back to Normal

Once the celebrating is over, get back to reality. Hopefully, you've learned some valuable lessons through this tough period in your life. Don't forget them.

There's a movie starring Burt Reynolds called *The End*. There's a scene I remember very clearly.

Burt is out in the ocean, way out. He was going to end it all, and then he changed his mind. As he is trying to swim to shore he doesn't think he will get there, and he believes he will drown. So he begins making deals with God about his survival. In the beginning, when things look their worst, he promises God that if he makes it to shore he will give up all his worldly possessions. As he continues toward shore and his confidence about surviving increases, his deals become less and less a sacrifice, until he finally reaches the shore, He proclaims, "Just kidding, God."

You get the point. When you were downsized and things looked their worst you probably made all kinds of deals. Hey, it's normal. However, now that you've landed a job, don't forget the deals you made.

Deals like: *I'll work smarter. I'll pay more attention to my subordinates and peers. I'll meet with people when they are trying to network. I'll pay more attention to my customers and go out of my way to realize that a company is built on personal relationships.* Keep those promises to yourself.

DON'T FORGET

Earlier in this book I mentioned that few people remember what pain feels like. **Remember the pain. Don't forget this part of your life.** It can make you a better person.

Learn from this period of your life – so that it doesn't happen again. Or, if it does happen again, make sure you go about finding a new opportunity the way you did this time, in a methodical, organized manner.

So, now that you have a new job or found that new opportunity, what are you going to do? Are you going to go back to the way things were? Please, don't. Your life will never be the same. Hopefully, it will be better. For sure, you'll be better.

You've acquired a vast amount of contacts through your networking system. What happens to them? Do you forget these people? No! These individuals were a great source of help and inspiration. Show them that you care.

Once you're back on the job, revisit all the names of the people you made contact with, whether those contacts were in person, via the telephone, letter, or e-mail. Send each and every contact a thank-you letter or e-mail. Tell them what you're doing, where you're located, and what your specific assignment is. If it's relevant, offer your new company's products or services to them. Most importantly, let them know that you're available to them for assistance whenever it is needed. It shows that you care. It also shows that you know that networking works both ways.

Several years ago when I was networking as a method to find new clients for my business, I was introduced to a person who recommended my company to do some strategic planning for a mid-market company.

It turned out to be a one-year assignment. I wanted to thank the referral, so I volunteered to conduct a workshop I do titled "Principles for Delivering Customer Delight" for his entire organization. I did the entire program for all of his employees, for free.

Since that time, he and I have become good friends, and he has referred at least five other companies to me. I've also referred customers to his organization. Everyone wins.

When things go bad and then become better, memories can fade. Make sure you don't forget this time. And do what you can to generate a positive business behavior.

But remember, no matter what you do, there may be circumstances beyond your control. You might experience unemployment again. No one can protect against it, even if you own and operate your own business.

Today's business environment is constantly changing – it's not your imagination – success is tougher then ever. That's why I recommend that as soon as possible, begin to take a personal inventory of where you want to be and how you will get there. For example, fewer individuals are qualifying for long-term company pension plans – so you may have to plan for retirement by yourself, using your own creative means.

If you don't have the knowledge, find someone who can help. The time is right now.

Don't wait for another setback.

Begin to develop a written strategy about your long-term future. If you rely on the company or on the government, you're relying on the wrong entity. Today you must rely on that person in the mirror.

Start now…the clock is ticking.

And celebrate the fact that you now have a new job or career opportunity. Enjoy the fact that, like millions of other Americans, you're in the workforce.

Even though millions of people say they can't wait for retirement, they don't want it to come too soon.

Enjoy the work that you do as you continue to be a productive asset within the American business system.

And maybe you'll be able to enjoy a vacation in the sun.

Congratulations, you'll have earned it!

Final Thoughts

"The two hardest things to handle in life are failure and success."

A Tougher Worker Enviornment

The threat of becoming unemployed continues to be a black cloud hanging over most American workers. Although at this writing, many say the economy is starting to move forward, many employees are hanging onto their jobs by a thin thread.

For example, fewer inside jobs are available. Companies will continue to utilize outside contractors as a means of saving money. Being able to save on benefit payments, healthcare costs, pension plan contributions, etc., is one way an organization can save on expenses.

Although most American workers believe that being an employee of a company is still the safest way to work, it is becoming increasing clear that, for many of us, some altered view about the work environment will need to take place.

I do believe that most manufacturing positions, the ones that stay, will continue to be filled by internal company employees. However, there will be many service-oriented positions now filled internally that will become outsourced. Many human resource functions such as payroll, accounting, and customer service will be farmed out to contractors. Some marketing positions will move outside. I'm sure you can name others.

Although that means new jobs for many people, it usually means that benefits provided internally will be eliminated in order to get a contract inexpensively, especially if the outside contractor is self-employed, a trend that seems to be occurring more often. Big business is trimming down.

While productivity numbers are on the increase, part of this means that workers currently employed are working harder, longer hours and must make up for those workers no longer employed.

Businesses continue to tighten their belts, and unemployment may well continue to be a major economic issue.

The Economic Atmosphere Is Changing

If you're one of those individuals relying on corporate America to give you a job and take care of you, as it was in the fifties, sixties, and even the seventies, forget it.

Those days are over. You may still have a job with one of these fine companies, but they're dealing with a different world, too. In today's business environment both companies and employees need to be creative and flexible. Many corporate employees are beginning to see the light and are either moving to smaller enterprises or going out on their own, either by themselves or with a partner or two.

I'm almost certain that entrepreneurial companies are growing much faster than most big businesses. Certainly that's where the new jobs are.

Although I don't mean this to be an indictment of big business, in many cases there appears to be too much internal politics, too much bureaucracy, too much indecision, too much overhead, too much nepotism, and not enough fun to lure future employees back to those environments.

Employees are beginning to put their family first again and are evaluating their current lifestyle to determine the direction they want to head. This evaluation should probably be done while you're employed. Many people wait too long – once they're downsized, reorganized, or part of a "reduction in force."

Anticipate Change and Prepare for It

Ladies and gentlemen, begin your evaluation process now.

If you're employed, don't wait until you're not. Panic could set in. You will not make realistic judgments, and your options will be more limited. The time to evaluate your lifestyle, career path, and where you want to go is when the pressure is off.

Read any newspaper, listen to any news program, and you can easily tell times are changing. The high-tech industry, the telecommunications sector, and many of their supportive industries have been decimated.

The computer segment of the economy and supportive industries are losing jobs to overseas countries that may offer much cheaper labor and still provide above-average performance.

Many of these countries are sending their citizens to America for education and training. Once completed, these individuals are going home and taking jobs with them. Is this right? I'm just asking the question.

My point in all this is that American workers must foresee these changes and prepare accordingly.

Many unemployed people, some of whom have been unemployed for some time, are beginning to change industries and, in some cases, disciplines. When this occurs, the networking process becomes more challenging. Here's why.

If you've worked in one industry for a number of years, your sphere of influence and contacts have probably been confined to that industry. If you're now trying to move outside that sphere, how do you go about making contact with individuals involved in the targeted industry? Try attending networking meetings where the attendees are in other industries. Make contact with individuals in your social circles who you know have acquaintances in other areas.

Back to the Basics

Back to the business environment.

In my humble opinion, if you want to fix what's wrong with the business environment, it doesn't take a genius to figure out you must concentrate on the basics, or go back to the basics if you left them. I'm fascinated by this. When businesses begin to get in trouble, what is one of the main reasons executives cite? "We moved away from the basics." If the basics are recognized as so important, why do companies move away from them?

My research shows that companies give the following reasons: *We bit off more than we could chew. We spent more time on the process than we did on meeting our customers' needs. We were so successful in one area we decided we could move into other areas, some of which we were not very adept* in. We made a decision to expand real fast to take advantage of market conditions, but we didn't realize that we grew faster than we could add qualified employees, thus we couldn't meet demand. Our customer support department was not trained in our new technology, and when customer complaints surfaced, we couldn't fix the problems. We grew too fast.

The list can go on and on for pages.

Staying Focused

Maybe I have an approach that's too simplistic, but if you want to reduce your chances of getting into difficulty, do the following: strategically determine your expertise, stay within your area of expertise, stick to your own basics, and do whatever it takes to delight your customer base.

Develop a written strategic plan for growth, just as you developed a plan for finding a new opportunity, refer to it often, stay alert if circumstances change. Make necessary changes and adjustments.

Several years ago I conducted an informal survey of some of my client's employees. I asked them, "What in your opinion is the biggest problem in your company?" Overwhelmingly, it was a **"lack of communication."** I find this very interesting since from a communication standpoint they had…voice mail, e-mail, caller ID, call forwarding, call waiting, cell phones, palm pilots, satellite locators, wireless e-mail, and more.

Today you can't go anywhere without seeing someone talking on a cell phone. You see them being used everywhere… in cars, on trains, in planes, in theatres, restaurants, places of worship, hospitals, supermarkets, department stores, shopping malls, sporting events, in health clubs while exercising, washrooms, while walking on the sidewalk, and yes, even in business.

My point is with all these devices why is communication still such a problem? I think I'll leave that one for you to ponder. I'm exhausted!

Years ago, everyone pointed fingers at the auto industry, saying it was not meeting the quality demands of the consumer. So what happened? American automotive sales plummeted. The auto industry began reducing the number of workers. The layoffs were massive. Thousands upon thousands of automotive workers were fired. Plants were shut down. Some towns were decimated. All this because customers were buying Japanese cars. Why? Because those companies listened to the American consumer and provided them what they wanted. They stayed with the basics. The American automakers didn't, and disaster followed.

Now the airline industry is in major difficulty. Why? Is it strictly because of the 9/11 catastrophe? No, they were floundering way before 9/11.

However, did you notice any senior airline executive stepping up to take responsibility for his company's poor performance and saying he would be accountable for his actions and respond accordingly?

Instead, the airlines supposedly "went back to basics" and fired or furloughed thousands of employees. For those who remained, their benefits and salaries were reduced. Was this an appropriate action? You be the judge. How did they get in such a situation in the first place, before 9/11?

In mid-2003 a study conducted by the Institute for Policy Studies and United for a Fair Economy reported that airline CEOs got raises amid cuts. The study showed that three major carriers "gave their CEOs raises after the September 11 terrorist attacks as they fired a total of 33,000 workers." And again, "As revenues plunged and the CEOs cut thousands of jobs, they received raises of $1.2 million to $3.4 million."

In one instance a CEO's total compensation package was 115% higher in 2003 than in 2001 when his company announced 17,000 employee layoffs. Now here's the amazing part of the story. It was reported that the same CEO wrote in a memo to employees that the pay raise in 2002 was approved before the terrorist attacks.

Does that mean that based upon the circumstances after 9/11 he could not have turned down or deferred the increase and shown some executive leadership? This is just another example of poor corporate accountability.

Before I conclude, I'd like to bring up one other point. Again, in my opinion, if you want to assist businesses in becoming profitable again, how about doing things that will improve consumer confidence? As employees continue to get laid off, what about punishing some of the corporate executives who are caught with their fingers in the pot?

(You know who they are.) Many of these corporate layoffs are due to unscrupulous executive behavior to begin with. Let's see what we can do to fix those problems.

Finally, let's begin to delight the customer again.

Not that long ago the customer was king or queen. If the customer had a complaint, it was handled with limited difficulty. You went back to the store of purchase or made a quick phone call and the problem was solved. Today if a customer has a problem it takes ten minutes to get through the automated telephone maze just to wait on hold for a real human being.

Hello Operator...Get Me Anyone

Let me provide an example. My computer was infected with the "Blaster" virus. I made a call to the help desk. I was directed to the website to download the fix. However, the virus didn't allow me to stay online long enough to download the remedy. I had to call a technician for help.

I called every hour on the hour for one solid day and received a message directing me to the website for the download, which I couldn't access. So I repeated that I had to talk with a technician. The next day at six o'clock in the morning I called the number and after several "press this number and press that number," I was told that my call would be answered soon. I was placed on hold and heard the same music until I fell asleep with the phone placed next to my ear.

Two Hours Later

Someone answered the phone, woke me up, and assisted me in fixing the problem.

Now you might be saying that's not so bad, it was a major problem affecting thousands and thousands of people. I was fortunate I was only on hold for two hours.

Remember, that was after I tried for an entire day to speak with someone. That to me is not fortunate or acceptable.

If you want to be successful, begin putting programs in place that will delight both internal and external customers. Believe me, if the customer is delighted, you'll be delighted.

Since everyone is a customer, there doesn't appear to be any downside to this scenario.

Let's begin to give the customer what they want and need, in an environment that is conducive to delighting them. If you can do that, your customers will definitely notice the difference. It's a sure way of surviving.

I know one thing for sure: if our current business environment changes soon, the unemployment picture will improve. Let's do everything we can to make sure that happens.

Well, this is THE END...or is it?